A W.

by the same author

SAGITTARIUS RISING
NEVER LOOK BACK

A WAY TO BE

Cecil Lewis

With an Introduction by
Colin Semper

COLLINS
FOUNT PAPERBACKS

First published in Fount Paperbacks 1977

© Cecil Lewis 1977
Introduction © Colin Semper 1977

Made and printed in Great Britain by
William Collins Sons & Co Ltd Glasgow

For K.B.
who saw the possibilities

Contents

Introduction

Is it not a fact that what really matters to us is mediated, not by abstract philosophical propositions or brilliant ideas but by personal meeting? The world's orphans receive little help from manuals of child care; they need mothers. The sick do not recover by reading a medical dictionary; they need the wielding of the scalpel and the healing touch of doctor and nurse.

Truth personalized. Argue, expound, express, discuss but it is truth incarnate in any personality which is most profound and mysterious.

It is for this reason that you must not just read the talks of Cecil Lewis. You must meet him. He is a giant octogenarian – nearly two metres tall, white well-trimmed beard, eyes that glint with life and living, love and anger. A big human being. Imperious. A leader – in the old tradition – before partnership or consultation came into fashion. Momentarily intimidating. Romantic, a streak of irresponsibility, loving but not always easy to love. Full of energy and, above all, a man wrestling 'until the breaking of the day', ever searching for a deeper understanding of his own reality, ever trying to relate what he does to who he is, ever convinced that lack of self-understanding bars the path between man and his possibilities.

It was this sort of man I saw; I mean it literally, for that is sometimes the way. He has since told me that he was fearful of the meeting. He thought that, being newly responsible for the places where his broadcasting fitted best, and being less than half his age, I should want to sweep away what he was trying to achieve. I had no such fear of the meeting for in my eight years at the BBC I had not heard another broadcaster who so excited me, compelled me to listen, often against my will, from day to day. The

9

chemistry worked and, in the face of a manic Christian propagandist, he even found that an *aggiornamento* of his activities was about to take place – even more he could, as he put it, 'peddle the esoteric Christianity'.

After eight years in religious broadcasting, I have come to the conclusion that it is much over-valued, particularly by the Christian laity. In my experience, not many lives are dramatically changed. Radio performances are transmitted in an intimate, conversational way and that is how they are received. Yet, there is a 'removed' quality about it; people rarely change as a result of what is said. Curiously, the more fiercely propagandist is the religious messenger, the more the economy of the medium of radio renders him counter-productive. Or, to put it more bluntly, proclaim as in preaching (and proclamation is the very nature of preaching) and switches are turned off. But there are some things which radio does superbly well, better than any other medium.

Not so long ago, I read a letter to a newspaper from a man who said that he had calculated how many sermons he had heard in his lifetime. The total came to several thousand, but, he declared 'I cannot remember a single one of them'. Next week there came a reply – 'I have been married to my wife for upwards of forty years. During that time she has cooked me thousands of meals. I cannot honestly remember a single one of them, but I still like her and I am still alive today.'

Radio feeds people well – it deals well with the abstract, the conceptual, the imaginative, the feelings. The choreography that the listener creates either of drama sets or the character of the human being is so much more impressive than the designer's work on cinema or television screens. So, if you will pardon the language, radio is good for religion. Unlike television, there is little paraphernalia to obstruct real communication and sound appeals to the one sense of hearing, and that very directly. This means that audience reaction of a significant kind is much bigger for radio than for television, at any rate in my area.

But radio is always transitory; I know that well. It is generally impulsive, quickly made, here today and gone the next minute. Whilst it is a truly creative medium, the machinery devours the product, and, alas, the machines proliferate. The number of outlets increases and the product is devalued. I am very sad about this. I could not live in the United States where there are six thousand radio stations. This means that endless signals compete for the attention and, in the end, nothing communicates because the listener's head is beaten to pulp by a variety of rubber hammers. In Britain, we seem to be following the USA. With all its limitations, I have come to care deeply about radio and if I should appear to be pleading for exclusivity, then so be it. And I prefer the confines of a broadcasting system where neither commercial interests nor government pressure or control corrupt and where thieves do not break through and steal.

This secular sermon has everything to do with Cecil Lewis. He was a founding father of a public service broad-casting company. His own broadcasts are quality – he will sit for hours and ponder a four-minute talk. This is not to say that he is going to pack many thoughts into a limited space, but that he is going to pack *much* thought into the expression, the translation, the communication of one thought.

What he says, he says simply and directly. But, I hope you will agree, the result is often profound. It is human too – invariably taken in essence from someone else and digested, made part of his own humanity and given from that humanity and experience to others.

If anyone would sift the spirit (to paraphrase Saul Bellow) in the public arena on radio, then it is only authentic humanity which will communicate, nothing else. Certainly not systematic theologies and philosophies which have remained in the head and which are fired at the general public. The thought must be in the stomach. The language must be simple and tailored. The expression must be subtle. The enthusiasm must be obvious. A sense of humour helps.

Because of the tremendous response of the listeners I

serve and in hope that the written word *can* really influence for change, I am emboldened to think that these broadcasts might make the journey from the spoken word to the written word.

It is a tribute to a broadcaster for his producer to be inundated with letters. In the case of BBC World Service the letters are worth a book in themselves. Few correspondents who trouble to send an airmail letter to London content themselves with simple sentences like 'I loved your programme'. They make comments, argue, vociferously disagree, challenge insularity, ask sharp questions. In the case of Cecil Lewis three questions predominate; how may I get in touch with him so that he may teach me, who is this man, and what sort of life has he led to be able to say these things? It is principally to this last question that I must finally turn.

Cecil Lewis came from non-conformity. His father was a Congregational Minister, a local Derbyshire leader of a church that is now merged with the English Presbyterian Church as the United Reformed Church. He was a good preacher and evidently filled his churches, for he was soon occupying the pulpit of one of Congregationalism's 'plums' – the King's Weigh House, Grosvenor Square, in the West End of London. There his conventional ministry ended and his so-called 'advanced' views were given opportunity for advancement. He felt that insecurity was implicit in the Christian way (it is) and that he should become a poor itinerant preacher and that 'God would provide'. A wealthy woman from the West End church said *she* would provide until the new life could begin. He married her and, to cut a painful story short, became utterly dependent and lived in a gilded cage having to ask for new clothing or even tobacco. He lived in sterile luxury for twenty years until he met a woman thirty years his junior who gave him back his self-respect, a daughter and a new life as a broadcaster of lay sermons, of pieces on words or customs or philosophy or theology.

Cecil Lewis' mother, whom he described as 'gay and courageous', lived a quiet, conventional life, remarried and, when her second husband died, married yet again. The latter half of her life seems to have been happy.

Cecil Lewis was sent to an English Public School – Oundle. To this day he remains grateful for the education, but though he could more than hold his own in the physical activity so central to a school like this, he was beset by an inner loneliness which bade him search for what is nobler, higher, inspired. In his autobiography *Never Look Back* (Hutchinson and Co.) he says 'It took me deep inside myself and set me apart, for I wished also to join the community of lonely ones who sang of this El Dorado of the spirit. But how could I sing if I did not know where or what it was? This secret longing has haunted me all my life.'

By the Christmas of 1915 he was a qualified pilot and commissioned in the Royal Flying Corps. In six months he had gone from school to the Front and those interested in early flying in the First World War can read of his exploits in *Sagittarius Rising* (Penguin Books). Suffice it here to say that flying above the trenches convinced Cecil Lewis that it is the 'invincible stupidity of men' that puts the future of our world in doubt.

After the end of the war, when he was twenty-one years old, he was offered instant adventure; he was to teach the Chinese to fly! The aircraft did not arrive and he was set loose in Peking for nine months to soak up the millenia of civilized Chinese life. It had a profound effect upon him and he believes that in China there is still the possibility of seeing a mould for the shape of future modern living. You will find echoes from his time in China in the broadcast talks; in particular what remains in his mind of a visit to a Buddhist monastery. 'If you could match this outer repose and peace with such an inner state you would have learned all there is to be learned. Nothing demanded or insisted, but everything called or pointed, clinging to the wayfarer, begging him to remember: there is something to be learned here. Enquire within.' (*Never Look Back*, op. cit.)

He received more from Peking – a Russian wife of noble birth – but ultimately felt that a European would always be an outsider in Chinese society, so he forsook the life of grandeur (the flying never really happened) and brought his new bride to broadcasting and to London.

It is fortunate that Cecil Lewis now lives in Greece. The only broadcasting he can hear and understand in its fullness emanates from the World Service of the BBC. The standards of quality that he helped to build as the first Deputy Director of Programmes of the BBC are still heard. There is little 'encroachment of the mediocre'. But gone, of course, is the pioneering excitement which enabled Cecil Lewis to harness the talents of the artists and entertainers of London in the twenties – Noel Coward, George Robey, Gertie Lawrence, Sybil Thorndike. He became friends with the painter Charles Ricketts RA and with George Bernard Shaw, both of whom had a tremendous influence upon him, giving him the largesse of their company, the benefits of their wisdom, the hilarity of their wit and the tolerance of parents at the outset of a rather mercurial career. (I paraphrase his own appreciation.)

There is an oft-repeated BBC programme-maker's saying that there are thousands of administrators stopping the programmes being transmitted. True or not, those of us who love making programmes repeat the accusation. Cecil Lewis felt it at the inception of broadcasting! He was idealistic and beset with that finest of Christian virtues, insecurity. Or, as he puts it, with the ideal of a 'do it yourself' life. He left the BBC and has 'done it himself' for the rest of his life, incurably romantic, attracted by adventure and emotion, making 'life decisions', as I call them, rather than those based on expediency. He was a film director, a Hollywood script writer, a South Sea Island beachcomber, a boat designer until, again, he took to the air in the Second World War.

By any standards he had a 'good' war – training pilots, informing the community of Air Force heroics, commanding staging posts. But this second dose left him asking big questions and with a sharp knowledge that he held no answers, no aims, no compass and no sense of direction. Furthermore, it seemed to him that no tried or established methods could bear fruit and that it was impossible, any-way, for the individual to achieve the miraculous. He was just about to abandon himself once more to action – to the design of a cruiser on which he would circumnavigate the globe – when a meeting changed all his plans and set him on the path which led him once more to the BBC, this time as a broadcaster.

He met a man, a man who fitted no category, who said to him – 'If you want to set the world to rights you must start by setting yourself to rights. Society is simply an aggregate of many you's and me's. Everything starts there. Until you have observed and accepted the wrong working of your own mechanism and understood it pretty thoroughly, you cannot hope to change it. You may not be able to do much about society, but you can do something about yourself. A few hundred ordinary men who understood themselves, i.e. *what they were really like*, could make a very considerable contribution to a different way of life for all mankind.' New wine had been poured into a middle-aged bottle. I am tempted to say – the wine has now fermented, the bottle is leathern and elderly but by no means in its dotage, so read on and you will see how the ideas of Georgi Ivanovitch Gurdjieff grasped a human being to such an extent that he lost all his possessions, and never doubted that here were answers which could satisfy modern man for many generations.

But I want to append a personal view. This 'work on oneself' is not for everyone. The basis – 'remember yourself always, everywhere' – appears simple but in truth is almost impossible. Of all men, Cecil Lewis knows this. What he writes is a struggle, the desperate venture of all faith. His entire humanity – including the Christianity of his up-bringing and the world faiths of his travelling – is focused in his 'translations' of what he calls 'the Work'.

Gurdjieff wrote much about the traditional means of the spiritual search. He recognized the hardship employed by the fakir, the love and vigil and devotion of the monk, and the power of the Yogi's mind.

But he felt that these methods had been over-used and

become threadbare. They must be included in a new dimension.

So Gurdjieff announced 'the fourth way' – a way which demanded that the body, the feelings, the head must be 'worked on', all at the same time. The fourth way is also the way of conscience; it is a way of finding direction for life *because of* the inner conscience. The fourth way depends upon what is called 'the staircase'. No one enters upon the fourth way straight out of life; that is impossible because there has been no leap into the religious life which a monk or nun might take. Life is to work on the self so that the climbing of the staircase begins. And at the top of the staircase stands the entrance to the way.

Cecil Lewis considers himself to be somewhere near the bottom of the staircase. He is still trying to climb towards the entrance to the way, which begins at a level above life.

The idea of 'the way' is, of course, ancient. Pliny used it in his letters to the Emperor Trajan when reporting the activities of the early Christians. I find that way utterly satisfying and I believe it gives me sufficient clues to living in this universe.

But it is a way that another has shown, has achieved, has *given* to me. Cecil Lewis acts out of his own strength; I act out of the strength of another. We are both wayfarers. Is it possible that we shall both appear at the threshold of the Kingdom of Heaven?

Colin Semper   January 1977
BBC – Religious Broadcasting
   (World Service)
Bush House, Strand
London

Chapter 1

Where We Stand

A hundred years ago the fastest thing on Earth was a galloping horse. Society lived at a corresponding pace. There was time for reflection, for discussion, for some hope of coming to reasoned decisions. Moreover the world was divided and subdivided in such a way that societies looked in on themselves, minded their own business and were, to a large extent, autonomous and self-supporting. This way of life produced communities with a wide range of differing personalities and permitted the flowering of the human spirit in a variety of ways, often so vivid, so appealing, that we prize the memory of it today as a fruit of the Golden Age.

All this has now been submerged by a flood of uniformity in which the individual has become more and more at the mercy of the mass. However much the world splinters up into smaller and smaller units, they all want the same thing. Science has telescoped space and time. What happens in Patagonia or the Moluccas is immediately known in Iceland and Hawaii. A Niagara of information pours over the world. Important or unimportant, dreadful or trivial, truth or rumour, it is all the same, part of a 'service', whose aim is that everybody should know everything.

The general effect of this is to saturate our receptive faculties. We can neither remember it nor take it in; but it fills us with frustration and anxiety. At the same time, if it is cut off for any reason, we feel lost and bored without it! So we develop a sort of love-hate relationship with the media which works itself out in a morbid curiosity about other people's misfortunes and an insatiable appetite for bad news.

This weathercock existence, swayed this way and that by everything that happens, is really the nub of our miserable existence. We are up to our necks in tensions and worries, most of which do not concern us; yet, at the same time these are almost evenly matched by the pleasures, comforts and distractions that go with it. So the pressing need to see where we are going withers in the ease that overlays it. Searching for some way to live with this only adds another worry. We long for everything to be simple, but it always turns out to be complicated. This makes us restless and nervous, yet we desperately long for quiet.

So we start 'taking' things. Drugs, to calm our anxiety or cure our depression, drugs to pep us up or make us relax, drugs to send us to sleep or keep us awake, drugs to stimulate or slow down almost every organ in the body. And if anyone dares to suggest that an inner discipline of body and mind would cure half the world's diseases, he is scoffed at as a mystic or a crank.

Yet through this global horror of killing and torture something else is beginning to emerge. Although we seem to be, collectively, quite devoid of morals, a glimmer of concern is starting to appear at the callous and brutal way we treat our fellow men. Disgust is beginning to get organized. Remorse, that revolt of one part of us against another, can be seen to be stirring. Conscience is being reborn.

But, for the moment, most of the time we opt out, go to ground and refuse to get involved. We shrink our interests to our personal affairs. A sort of numb egoism envelops us. Maybe we should feel this or that, help here or there; but, in general, it is too difficult, too complicated. This is the real battleground, the David and Goliath of our lives, the tiny twinge at the way things are faced with the giant inertia of don't care and don't want to know. Young David needs a new weapon if he is to win.

But is there such a weapon? Is there any way out except through some Armageddon of global destruction? After which, if there is anything left, a new start can be made. Many think not. The old game of power politics, of pacts, treaties, summits and such like, is the only way we know to stave off catastrophe. Their efficacy is, at best, extremely doubtful. At some point it will prove irresistible to use the weapons before they become obsolete.

All attempts to simplify the complex get out of focus and this thumbnail sketch of our current dilemma is certainly no exception. At the same time it may convey, however crudely, the drift of ideas which many share, namely that 'things' are far from right. They have become sufficiently disturbed to begin to give serious attention to any ideas which offer some hope of 'making sense' of their situation, or, better still, to find some way out of it.

I think there are, and always have been, ways out for those who have the need. But these 'ways' must always have a certain correspondence, a certain affinity, with the mode of thought, the attitude to life, that prevails at that time. With the passing of years, truths become distorted and overlaid with comment and dogma, obscuring and even contradicting what was first given. At the same time the temporal scene changes, need degenerates into habit, so polluting the source itself and making it tasteless.

Knowing the inevitable cycle, it seems that Compassionate Forces above and outside life, bring down to earth from age to age individuals who may be called Sacred Messengers, and who embody, in human form, the essence of Divinity. Their task is to show, by their own example, that another way of life is possible and to give powerful indications to all those who, under their influence, begin to aspire to such a life. But, above all, they touch the quick of the age, diagnose the disease, and propose a cure which can return the sufferer to health.

Towards the end of the nineteenth century just such a man was born in a remote town in eastern Turkey, the son of a carpenter. As a boy he showed exceptional natural endowments and began, at an early age, to conceive a burning desire to investigate all sorts of 'supernatural' phenomena which he noticed in the world around him. He became convinced that, behind them, must lie hidden truths, hidden powers, which had once been known to man, but were now lost. Drawing a number of like-minded young men round him, the group began to search for the sources of these truths, penetrating through all manner of hazards and difficulties, into the remotest parts of Africa, India and Asia. From these intensive searches (which lasted over twenty years) he finally came to Moscow and began to transmit a synthesis of all he had found and understood to groups of people who were drawn to him. Forced by the Revolution to leave Russia he came west to Europe and finally settled in Paris, where he died in 1949.

The range and scale of the 'ideas' which he, as he put it, 'imported into life', is vast. He proposed a new conception of the birth of the Universe and set out the fundamental laws by which it continues to be created and maintained. Gradually the plan of an ordered, structured Cosmos, in all its immensity and variety, begins to emerge, within which we grains of sand have nevertheless our place and purpose. Woven through all this is a deep and intimate dissection of our human nature, its frailties and its possibilities, which compels us to begin to face our situation and to realize what is required of us if we are to fulfil the destiny for which we were created.

· Embroidered and embellished with a thousand tributary motifs and designs, his master work, *All and Everything* in *Beelzebub's Tales to his Grandson*, by G. I. Gurdjieff (1950, Routledge, Kegan Paul Ltd) contains a new vision of the nature of the Mystery within which we find ourselves and the sense and aim of our life within it. This is the teaching of Gurdjieff, a legacy of such power and depth, it cannot fail to be a beacon in the world to come.

Around Gurdjieff's work a nucleus has formed, some of whom studied with him, of people who are gradually and carefully beginning to spread his ideas in many parts of the world. At the same time, inevitably, splinter groups, ignoring the disciplines and dangers, have begun to use and misuse his work. Books setting out to explain and teach what he taught have already appeared and many more will certainly follow. All that can be said in this one – and I wish it to be clearly understood – is that, although I have studied with those close to Gurdjieff for thirty years, I do not presume to 'teach' anything; but simply to share a few crumbs from his work that I think I have understood. But all the inspiration behind this collection of short essays derives directly or indirectly from the teaching of Gurdjieff. It is *he* who touches you, if you are touched.

Today in the West, the Church has got bogged down in much that is empty and hypocritical and this has effectively turned people away from serious contemplation of subjects which concern them. But there is, in fact, a great deal in the 'foothills' of what we call 'religion' that is plain common-sense and enlightened self-interest and which loses by being daubed with a 'holy' brush. The fact that our understanding of life, as it grows and deepens, inevitably leads us towards mysteries that are not understandable is no reason whatever for us never to question or try to understand anything at all.

I would be glad for these short 'talks' broadcast over the past two or three years in the World Service of the BBC, to be considered rather like those entertainers, fiddlers, jugglers, and the like, who enliven our theatre queues. They are not so good as what you may expect to find inside; but they are in the same vein, so to speak. Their aim has been nothing more than to help us all – myself thoroughly included – to wake up to our situation, to both our stupidities and our possibilities in coping with life and to struggle to find some way out of the quagmire on to solid ground.

Above all I would entreat the reader who has embarked upon this book *not* to attempt to read it through like a novel. Between these broadcast talks, given at daily intervals, there was always time for a listener to reflect and come back on the day following with a sense of refreshment. Many of the ideas contained in these pages are strange and new. They need to be digested. There is nothing consecutive about the order in which they are presented, so it is best to dip into the book at random. In this way it may be possible to obtain some benefit – and this alone matters.

Chapter 2

What is Religion?

I

Is there any value in what we call 'religion'? What is religion anyway? Do I need it? Or do I only imagine I need it? If I need it, what is the need it satisfies? If it helps me, how does it help me? Am I 'better' for it? What do I mean by 'better'? Better in my own eyes? Better with my fellow men? Better in my work, better in difficult situations? How better?

It seems to me that these are very interesting questions. Questions we never ask ourselves. We take all this 'for granted', as we say. Probably because we were brought up with the idea that there was a 'God' who somehow directed our lives and to whom we owed a certain respect and allegiance. But how He did this, and why, were never very clear – to me, at any rate. And I think it may not be clear to a lot of people.

In fact there are men – highly intelligent and able men – who deny the idea of 'God' altogether. Two big countries on our planet, Russia and China, have repudiated any need for religion, have struck it out of the social structure as unnecessary – and worse. This is all medieval nonsense, they say. Man is perfectly capable of working out his own destiny and the idea that there are mysterious forces above him and beyond him is just passing the buck to excuse his own mistakes. Our business, they say, is with this life, not some hypothetical life to come, and to allow society to be hoodwinked, sidetracked, into such dreams, is wasteful, dangerous, and stops them getting on with their jobs.

This idea that religion is a luxury, a luxury we don't need and cannot afford – and, moreover, a luxury that collides head-on with a practical approach to life by introducing quite another scale of values – is not so far wide of the mark.

Ask yourself, you who are listening to me at this moment, how much time, how much thought, do you give to religion every day? Three minutes? Four minutes? I assure you that even if you give it this, you are already an exceptional person. The majority of us go weeks, months, years, without giving it more than a passing thought. Your immortal soul is a luxury – like chocolate creams or a pint of beer – something you don't actually *need*, but is rather fun to indulge, from time to time.

Life today, after all, is a serious, frustrating, and rather depressing business. Why should we add to our difficulties by posing a whole new series of unanswerable questions?

But, all the same, there must have been, down the ages, some need that people felt, otherwise 'religion' would never have caught on at all. But how did it come about? What is it?

II

Modern society has done quite a lot to insulate us from the natural world in which we live. We have learned to keep the fluctuations of the seasons at bay, to maintain a sort of equilibrium. To a large extent we feel we have conquered, or 'tamed' Nature.

But in primitive, tribal societies, there was no question of anything like this. A good harvest to the farmer, a good catch for the fisherman, was essential. Without them people would starve or die. But it was perfectly clear that getting these essentials didn't entirely lie in a man's own hands. He couldn't control the weather. There were forces, far more powerful, that played a decisive role in his life. Storms or droughts, floods or gales, spelt disaster. More equable seasons spelt plenty.

When you live very close to the forces of Nature, it is almost impossible not to believe, when they are violent, that they are directed against you, personally. From this it is only a step to believing that these forces are wielded by someone who is either a friend or an enemy and who helps or hinders you according to the way you behave. So you offer gifts to your friend in gratitude for what he has given you – but you offer even greater gifts if he has been unfriendly and needs to be placated.

From this idea whole pantheons of gods and spirits were dreamed up by man to try to reach some sort of relationship with forces he didn't understand, which were far 'above' him, and yet vitally affected his life. Parallel with this grew up the idea that man's personal behaviour could, in turn, please or displease these 'gods'. So he began to create rituals, sacrifices, ceremonies, dances, to induce the conditions he required.

Today, of course, we know that although these forces certainly exist and exert a great influence on our lives and behaviour, they are not the unpredictable whims of 'gods', but the action and reaction of natural forces following laws, which, although we don't fully understand them, are not 'personal' forces meted out for our good or bad behaviour. But the idea, which was born in this way, that there were mysterious higher influences which somehow affect the human destiny, has remained.

This world of spirits and gods which man evolved to explain what he could not otherwise explain, became so real to him that he began to imagine relationships between the gods of this 'higher' world. He began to give them attributes. There were men and women gods. Some were greater than others, and there was, of course, a 'chief', who ruled them all.

Today we see the whole concept as nonsense. So why hasn't 'religion' – as we have grown to call this category of ideas – died out altogether? How has it managed to survive at all in this day and age? Is there some other ingredient?

III

Generally speaking, these gods that man created in his own image, were more against him than for him. When things were going well, he imagined them to be resting or sleeping or busy elsewhere. When they intervened, it always seemed to be in anger or jealousy or vengeance. Anger or vengeance against what? Against poor man for transgressing some laws he didn't understand. Or simply for not offering big enough presents. So he began to pile it on. His finest stock, his first-born children. At first sight there seems to be something degrading about this self-abasement.

But, in fact, it is not quite like this, for somehow another ingredient began to come into what we call 'religious belief' and that was human *aspiration*. For some reason man aspired to be other than he was. He got the idea that he was capable of being 'better'. It is a very curious attribute. Animals do not have it. A dog does not aspire to be a better dog, or a spider to be a better spider. It is only human beings who have somehow acquired this uncomfortable, nagging idea that they are not as they should be.

So, somewhere along the lines, man accepted this very strange idea, which no other living creature has, that he was imperfect. This sense of imperfection took various forms. One side of it was practical, vocational. He could aspire to be stronger, to shoot an arrow straighter, to be more skilful in the crafts of life, to be what we should call today more 'efficient'. That was a personal, partly ambitious, instinctive aspiration. To be cock of the walk is an animal attribute, part of the survival of the species, something men do for their own ends.

But there were also two other aspirations. Both were concerned with attitudes. He had to find a right attitude to these gods he wanted to please and, since he rarely lived alone but formed part of a community, he had to find an attitude towards his fellow men, since they too were searching for an answer to these questions.

Out of all this new factors began to emerge. Some people seemed to be more lucky or more intelligent in this search. They began to set themselves up as witch doctors, priests, leaders who asserted that they *knew* what would please the gods. They began to invent codes of behaviour to which they forced others to conform.

So now man had added a second set of burdens to his life. To begin with he hadn't known how to please the gods, and now he didn't know how to please the priests! And because these priests who had set themselves up to be intermediaries between man and his gods were closer, their authority became greater.

So, all over the world, various religious rituals were evolved, some honest, some corrupt; but all of them authoritarian, claiming that they *knew* and that their way was the only way to lead a virtuous life. So, because many good men are simple, their instinctive aspirations were often imperfectly answered without their knowing it and the last state was worse than the first.

IV

We have been speaking, so far, of simple, primitive societies groping to relate to powers greater than their own, recognizing, first that there was something 'above' them and second, that there was something inside themselves which urged them to reach upwards towards these higher powers.

Although at various times in various parts of the world more sophisticated ideas developed, these two streams – involution and evolution – man reaching up and God reaching down, remain the essential basis of all religions.

The sophistications, the developments, in all this grew slowly. When men reached the stage of having the leisure to ponder on life, they began to see that these natural forces which were so important to them, were only the foreground, so to speak, to greater a..d more majestic powers which held the planets in their orbits and set the galaxies whirling in the infinite depths of space. From being all important, unique, the centre of the Universe, man found himself shrinking and shrinking till he was forced to admit he was less than a gnat in the cathedral of life. He began to postulate, beyond the streams and floods, a Being, infinitely more powerful than these lesser gods. The comfortable father figure grew into the Great Originator, the Uni-Being Creator, the Prime Source of Everything Existing.

Yet these infinite complexities, and his own infinite nothingness, did not and do not remove his own personal problem. However unimportant, he has still to live his life. How best to live it?

It is all too easy, faced with the picture we have of the world today, to shrug the whole thing off. Do you never feel, as I do, a sort of vertigo when you consider your own position? We tiny human beings seem poised between two precipices. Below is the abyss of the infinitely small, the virus, the electron; above lies the maw of the infinitely great, the whole Universe exploding at the speed of light. How can anything we do, or do not do, possibly have any importance whatever in this devouring vortex of life which sucks us all into oblivion? We dare neither look down nor look up without a feeling that if we do, we shall lose our balance and be lost.

Better perhaps not to look at all! For, at the end of the day, how do the electron microscopes and the radar telescopes help us in the living of this life, which is all we have? Fascinating speculation blinds us with science; but it only baffles and perplexes us. It does not help. Here and now is our concern. For what can we do but accept our place, however small? We shall be no nearer to a solution of our human fate by measuring the orbits of the galaxies or the speeds of alpha particles.

If we make these things our gods, they will finally drive us mad – in fact it often seems they have done so already.

V

Elemental forces and higher laws impinging on man's life and, often subconsciously, steering him in this or that direction, all these are difficult abstract ideas. It becomes far easier if they are personalized. Poseidon stirs up the oceans, Thor throws the thunderbolts. Even when man evolved to a wider understanding, he called the author of it all the 'Father'.

One of the reasons why established religions have lost their grip on us is that we can no longer accept this cosy, fairytale attitude to life. Science has made it impossible.

Today we are forced to see life as the interplay of immensely complex forces which become more and more strange and intricate the more we probe them.

As human beings we simply cannot relate to all this. What do the galaxies care about me? How can I care about the millions of cells in my own body? But the galaxies and the cells are also part of the facts of life. So there must be a relationship. And of course there is. It is a question of scale. I have my place on the ladder of life and can do no more than struggle to understand it. But, for the moment, we must leave that aspect aside.

When we have unravelled the mysteries of the double helix and the paradoxes of the 'black holes', the secrets of life and death remain inviolate. They cannot be 'explained'. They cannot be answered. Here we are with our lives, surrounded by enigmas, as we have always been. They are different maybe; but just as baffling, just as real.

Faced with all this, some people refuse the idea that there is any destiny for us beyond this existence. They deny there is any immortal part which inhabits us and can persist beyond our own extinction. All this, they say, is just a sentimental hypothesis, impossible to prove, which feeds our egoism. At the other end there are those who believe in a God that cares for them; in Heaven; in the resurrection of the body and in the possibility of a personal, immortal life. Between these two lies the vast majority who cannot accept either of these extremes and have given the whole thing up as a bad job. When they think about it – if they think about it – they get muddled and frightened. Nobody knows the answers. Better not to tangle with it, better to leave it alone.

But among these lies another small minority, who do not give up so easily. Nothing seems to make sense, true; but it *must* make sense. We see laws all about us; laws of evolution and involution, laws of gravity, laws of motion, laws of relativity. In spite of the complexity, it is a rational ordered universe in which we live. Impossible then that there should not also be laws which govern the human destiny, laws to which we personally can relate. But what are they? This is our search.

You remember how Jesus put it in the Sermon on the Mount? 'Blessed are they that hunger and thirst after righteousness for they shall be filled.'

VI

So, to end this short enquiry into the question: what is religion? I think we can say, religion is an attitude to life. It is a way to *be* towards all the complexities and vicissitudes to which we are subject. It is a way to *be* before the beauty and wonder of the world. It is a way to *be* before our own contradictions and failings.

What is this attitude? How should we BE? When we look around for inspiration to the lives of men and women who seem to have found an attitude we can respect and aspire to ourselves, what do we find? Certainly not ambition or lust for power or material things. Certainly not greed or pride or selfishness. Such people seem to be set apart from the rest of us by living a life according to quite another set of values. They do not criticize or insist. They do not dictate or judge. The storms of life run off them like water off a duck's back. They do not get wet under the floods of worry and perplexity that soak us to the skin. They are free because they do not want anything for themselves. They listen more than they speak. They watch. They hope. They help.

What is it that we really want? Surely it is to be more adjusted to our difficulties, to be free of the contradictions that we see inside ourselves. For, even if we obtained a five-minute interview with God, we should still have to return to our lives, to our human problems. Nobody – not even God – can solve those for us. We have to solve them for ourselves. This is how we can struggle. This is how we can grow to be free of them. There is no other way to freedom.

So we really do not need to bother our heads about 'higher matters'. Neither the nature of God or Divinity, nor the marvels of science need phase us. Everything is here; inside us, around us. Know yourself and you will know God. The Kingdom of Heaven is within us – and so are all the contradictions, all the fears, all the failings. We have to sort it out. And, when we are lost we can turn – if we are lucky – to draw inspiration and help from those who have struggled and sorted it out a bit better than we have.

At the end it is all very simple. Do you know the epitaph that Gurdjieff asked any disciples of his who could find his father's unknown grave, to carve upon it? Here it is:

> I am Thou.
> Thou art I.
> He is ours.
> We are both his.
> And all shall be
> For our neighbour.

Chapter 3

What Do You Believe In?

I

What do you believe in?

It's a searching question, isn't it? And one which most of us, if we were asked seriously and in private, would probably shrug our shoulders and answer 'Nothing!' or 'I don't know.' Only a fortunate minority today lead a life illuminated by belief.

What has happened? How has it come about? Well, it seems to me, a great change has come over the world in the last 200 years. In the old days, God was seen as a loving Father, who cared for and watched over each of us personally, who took an active interest in all that was going on and who, if the old Adam in us sinned or fell from Grace, was ready to offer us – after suitable penitence – mercy, forgiveness and absolution.

Even as I say this, I can't help feeling how much our attitudes have changed. It almost sounds like a fairy-tale. It belongs to a time when life was far simpler and more naïve than it is today. It was none the worse for that. There is a cloud of witness throughout art and architecture to the purity and sincerity of faith that such beliefs inspired. And now? It seems we are all cynics. The homespun truths of yesterday are scorned; the devout works of art an excellent investment. What need is there for religion? The Open University explains things much better. What has happened to us all? It seems to me that our *way of thinking* has changed.

We are privileged – or cursed – it depends on your point of view – to be living in one of the great transitional periods of history. Everything is in flux, changing, flying apart, at an accelerating pace. It is all bewildering, frightening, dangerous – and challenging, stimulating, thrilling at the same time. Science has kicked the top of the world's ant-hill and the whole nest is seething. Everything is breaking up. Ideologies, philosophies, morals, habits, they are all in question. Wherever you look, yesterday's right is today's wrong, yesterday's good is today's evil.

The anarchy of all this, the suffering, the fear, the question mark under which we all live, cries out for help, for something to hold on to. But there seems to be nothing. Or is there?

The material provokes the spiritual. Parallel with the disasters, dissatisfied people, mostly young people, have started to search, probing every corner, from Tibet to Mexico, from drugs to transcendental meditation, to find some answer – for answer there surely must be – What is true? What can I believe in?

New things certainly have been found; but in a curious way they seem incomplete. Either they have been borrowed from ways of life fundamentally strange to the West or else they focus on personal salvation against no solid background. We need more than this. We are small pieces in a very large jigsaw; but we have a place in the Almighty Puzzle, and a rightful place, and we need to know where it is, however insignificant it may be.

So, to change the metaphor, we need an up-to-date map of the mountain and a good guide to show us the new way up. But where is all this to be found?

II

If we are to find a new way up the mountain, then, obviously, we must look in another direction. Something other worldly, outside life, no longer helps us. That belongs to the past. We are seeking something *valid for our time*.

And our time contains something that has never existed before, something entirely new, which may broadly be called a 'scientific approach' to life. Our civilization is dominated by a wealth of new techniques. We don't understand a hundredth part of them, but they colour our thinking. The world of astro-physics and genetic engineering is a closed book to us; but we begin to get a glimpse of some universal order, very big or very small, but uniform, subject to law. Hundreds of machines of astonishing ingenuity and complexity serve us and condition us, almost without our knowing it, to notions of scale and structure, of stress and speed. We cannot dismiss all this as mere technology, mystique. It has become a new component in our speech and thought.

Until all this happened, religious belief – and all thought about such belief – arose from men's *feelings*. The mind was left out of it, put to sleep, as soon as these feelings were touched. No matter how unbelievable these tales of the sun standing still or the waters being parted, of pillars of fire or burning bushes, they were all swallowed whole, taken at their face value, as fact. It was blasphemous to question them even.

And then, about 200 years ago, imperceptibly at first, but soon 'like a Jericho trumpet in crescendo', men began to think, to question everything, to put all religious belief in doubt. No longer was anything to be taken on trust, no longer was anything sacred. A merciless pragmatic search to 'get to the bottom of things' became the order of the day. Anything that could not be 'proved' was thrown out, fit only for the dustbin. This is our situation today and the suddenness and force of the scientific assault has knocked our spiritual life sideways.

But the sacred does not disappear from life just because a few earnest boffins start blinding us with science about 'mini black holes' or 'alpha particles'. God is not mocked so easily as that.

The question is – and it is a vital, burning question – where is the New Sacred that can replace the Old Sacred? How can we find a formula, a discipline that, based on eternal truths, does not ask for blind faith; but can stand up to questions in the market-place from thoughtful men? If there is something 'beyond', we must be led to it by logical steps we can accept. Is it possible, given the wide divergence of the material and the spiritual – and the way the bullying arrogance of facts stifles the still small voice – is it possible to find some key to a new harmony, even unity, that would inspire a 'revaluation of all values'?

That, it seems to me, is THE question.

III

This 'revaluation of all values', is, I think, a basic need of our age. We stipulate that before we can accept anything we have the right to know the how and why of it. The Prime Source we call God is largely discredited today because we cannot in any way relate it to modern terms. God is all right in a flower, but not in a computer; in a bird, but not in Concorde. It is all because we are stuck with this medieval picture of the Almighty as an old man with a beard, who is swanning about somewhere 'up there', but seems totally irrelevant to our current situation.

But to throw out the whole concept of Divinity because the old man with a beard won't wash, is to throw out the baby with the bathwater. After all, the old man is *our* idea. Somebody once told us we were created in God's image and we have been repaying Him the compliment ever since. I cannot believe in Michelangelo's vision of God the Father on the roof of the Sistine Chapel just because it happens to be an artistic masterpiece. It spoke majestically to its time: today its message is not appropriate.

There is another striking hangover from this naïve way of thinking and that is the idea that there is nothing between God and us. The galaxies, the spiral nebulae, the billions of suns, the visiting comets, all these are nothing – just white hot cannon balls whirling round in a vacuum – and God comes wading through this sparkling ether to listen to our petition for a good harvest or for the destruction of our enemies – which are certainly not His. All this needs re-thinking surely? Are we that important? Where is our sense of scale?

You remember the Lord's question to Job? 'Where was thou when I laid the foundations of the Earth?' Where were we indeed with our little understanding. Long before the human race existed the motions of the star were calculated, set. The solar systems swung in the womb of the galaxies, keeping their station in gravitational fields of immense complexity. Did all this phase of the Creation happen by itself? It is impossible to believe it. Left to itself everything runs down. To maintain itself life must be ordered, governed. Without government, chaos – as we see very well today. But who keeps the order? By what wonders of the intelligence were these interlocking orbits created? By what breathtaking dexterity are they maintained without interference or collision? It is a miracle. God is, among other things, the arch Astro-Physicist of the Universe.

But if we think of the God of the pretty pictures and fairy-tales as naïve, the non-god of the communists, materialists and atheists, is equally childish. These are not the alternatives. Can we not recognize the Divine Intelligence? Surely we can see, in every branch of science – chemistry, biology, physics, that wherever we touch reality, we find structure, order, harmony – all related with incredible delicacy and subtlety. We have to thank science for showing us that.

So, if we are to find a New Sacred to replace the Old, there must be room in it for Reason and Order, as well as Love. 'In the beginning was the Word!'

IV

So we must begin to grow up. The old picture of the kind of world we live in no longer tallies with the way we see it today. Our mode of thought has changed and, as a result, we question all our old beliefs. Many wonder whether any belief at all is necessary. But those of us who search look for a new structure which corresponds to the nature of reality as we see it and to which we can relate our personal longings to understand. Once we find such a structure we begin to feel safe within it. We can go forward having found our place, a place in which we, so to speak, 'mesh' with everything we meet. We cannot be surprised, uncertain or dismayed because all our experiences can be related to known points of reference and seen to fit.

Now this is, of course, a wonderful reassurance, a source of strength and hope; but it is not enough by itself. To return to our old metaphor of the mountain. It is certainly useful, essential even, to have a good map of your route. But climbing is another matter. For that you need a stout heart, staying power and a good pair of boots. But all that side we must leave for another time . . .

Before we set out on such a journey into unknown country, it is advisable to study the way, to get some idea of the lie of the land, so to speak. And this takes time, a lot of time even.

Thirty years ago I met and began to study the teaching of Gurdjieff – a master of whom few of you will have heard, I expect; but whose work will certainly steadily increase its influence throughout the world. After such a time I am fairly familiar with the outlines of the structure of the reality he suggests and I feel at home in it. Most of you are not, so, as it corresponds very well, I feel, with the needs of today, I would like to leave you with a few of his lines of thought to ponder and question:

There is, first, the Most Holy Prime Source, the Uni-Being Creator, and the two Primordial Sacred Laws by which the Will of the Absolute is maintained throughout the Universe.

There is the Divine Love of God which, like Time, flows everywhere and permeates the essence of everything that exists.

There is the Structure of the Universe, concentric worlds within worlds. From the Whole to the Atom, each is a self-sustaining Cosmos, similar to those above and below. Man also is such a world and it is in this sense that he is made in the image of God.

We inhabit a dark, remote corner of the Universe and our struggles and difficulties are proportional to our distance from the Centre.

God has need for those who struggle as much as they have need of Him.

Everything, without exception, in the Universe is

material. We lack only the instruments fine enough to measure the Spirit and weigh the Soul.

The root of all sin is sleep. Therefore struggle to awake and remember yourself always, everywhere.

We must strive to understand. This alone can lead us to the Lord God.

Chapter 4

Is There Anybody There?

The simple answer, as far as I am concerned, is 'Yes!' But the question has at least two aspects. First, is there Someone to whom I can put personal questions and get useful answers, a sort of direct line to the Almighty on my problems? Second, is there a Prime Source of Everything Existing in the Universe who created all there is?

In fact, the second aspect of the question contains the first. Many would insist that the Author of Everything Existing cares for the whole of it – and that includes me. I therefore have a direct personal link with Him. For my part, I must frankly admit I have no personal experience of situations in which I can discern the intervention of God 'on my side' to change the outcome. I know there are many instances of what appears to be 'help' in emergencies great and small. But it seems to me that it depends very much what the emergency is and the 'weight' of the thought of the suppliant. Alas, our feather-weight thoughts don't usually get far beyond petition of one kind or another and though such requests may occasionally seem to be answered, it must be acknowledged that there are ten thousand similar petitions, uttered with equal fervour, that are not. My difficulty is that I cannot accept the idea that God is inconsistent. I cannot think of Him as whimsical. I attribute to Him an *attitude*, a constant attitude, towards His Creation. If He can permit the horrors of Belsen and Auschwitz, how can He let me off the hook in some personal agony? I simply don't believe it can work like that.

Of course the 'long arm of coincidence' throws up strange, unexpected 'miracles', the weaving of the processes of life are extremely complex. There are also 'influences', the striking way one person can affect the life of another. But, in general, I see no reason to suppose the Laws of God will be twisted in my favour. In perhaps not quite the obvious way, I shall get what I deserve, and must accept it.

Some of you may feel that this is the attitude of an 'unbeliever' and that not to consider God the Father as a friend and adviser is heresy. My difficulty here may strike you as curious: it is one of scale. It is the outcome, I suppose, of what is called the 'scientific attitude'. Today we know so much about the nature of life, the way it is organized in its greater and smaller dimensions, we see how marvellous, magnificent and *ordered* it is at every level, we can no longer reduce the Prime Source to the level of an intimate family friend. That is really too smug, too cosy. It doesn't relate to our understanding of the nature of the world we live in and it is for reasons of this kind that traditional religion, churchgoing and the rest of it, has broken down. All the same most of us earnestly desire to have something we can wholly believe in, the problem is to find something that will relate God to our world and *make sense*.

That, at any rate, was my problem and it smouldered away inside me for many years: how to reconcile all the materialistic views of the modern world with the Divine Creator of it? Reconcile is too easy a word. I mean meld, weld, synthesize, until the two were inextricably, inevitably one. At last I found this in the teaching of Gurdjieff.

What I began to learn from this teaching was not only a categoric affirmative to the question 'Is there anyone there?'; but an awe-inspiring and comprehensive vista as to the nature of the Universe and how it was, so to speak, put together; how everything related to everything else, great and small; how there was an ordered proliferation of the apex All to the base Everything; how the greater contained the less; how the Divine Inspiration of the Prime Source caused the Great Cosmos of the Universe to be created and set up Laws to prevent its ever being destroyed by Time.

My problems as to the *Nature* of all life – including my own – were solved. How to orientate myself to it all, how to *be* in the rush of the traffic, that is another matter, unsolved and maybe never wholly solvable. But to those who have not so far been so fortunate as to find such a lifeline, I realize that fundamental questions remain, such as:

Is there anyone to replace dear old God, the Father? Is there a Central Intelligence, a Great Originator, a Uni-Being Creator, masterminding the Super Novae and the DNA, controlling the orbit of the Milky Way and the mutations of the gametes, or is there not? Is everything the mindless result of everything else, a self-perpetuating chain of cause and effect? Or is there some purpose, some direction in which all life is pointed? Is there anyone there?

Many say No. Two large nations have, officially, banished all idea of supernatural powers. Man is master of his own fate, captain of his own soul and to introduce any authority other than the temporal is to set up double standards, wasteful, divisive and dangerous to their authority.

Many others say Yes. There is a Creator, a Divine Authority, the Inspiration of all life. But today, it is not enough to affirm it because your father, or tradition, or the Bible, has laid it down. Nor is it enough to brush aside all anomalies and contradictions with Job's emotional cry: 'I *know* that my Redeemer liveth.' Today Reason must also be satisfied. We need proof. Head, heart and instinct must all agree. But can there possibly be any proof?

The scientists have a very fair approach to such problems. When they observe a number of related phenomena, they look for some underlying hypothesis that could unify them. Gradually, as more facts emerge, they refine the hypothesis and, if it holds up, the theory becomes firm enough to be called a Law. But here we are looking for universal laws, wide and deep enough to be ascribed to the Divine Governor of Everything Existing. Can we find any such laws?

Have you ever noticed a very simple fact, so simple it is easily overlooked, that in every happening, every event, large or small, inside or outside our lives, there are always three forces, three ingredients? For example, listening to a broadcast, there is the transmitter, your receiver and the carrier wave that brings the speaker's words to you. Without the carrier, the third ingredient, there could be no contact between us. Similarly, I speak, you listen, but the *speech*,

which relates us, is neither me nor you. It is the same with
everything. Artist, music, audience, makes the event of the
concert. Father, mother, children, make the event of the
family. How many chemical compounds cannot combine
without a catalyst? What holds the moon in orbit round
the Earth if not the gravitational force that relates the two?
This is the nature of reality.

We do not live, as we have too long imagined, in a dualistic world, you and me, black and white, hot and cold, right
and wrong. To limit our thinking in this way is to miss the
essential nature of reality and to live in a world of illusion.
All serious religions, in some form or other, have always
begged Man to free himself from the 'opposites'. This is
why, at the fountain-head of the Christian tradition, stand
the Father, the Son and the Holy Ghost. This is why all
religions, under various names, have postulated a Trinity.
Such a law as this, so simple, fundamental and all-embracing,
is sufficient alone for us to postulate a Divine Principle.
Such an hypothesis, supported by so many observed facts,
cannot have arisen 'by itself', it can only spring from law,
from the creative love of God.

Why do I bring love into it? Because I don't think anything can be created without it. Find me the artist who does
not feel, in the act of creation, a surge, an impulse of joy,
towards his creation. Later he may strut and show off, but,
at the outset, there is, must be, a spark of love towards
the thing he is about to create. And, when we turn to
Nature, he must be a dullard indeed who can ignore the
beauty and diversity of it all. Joy and love well from every
pore of it. Has all this happened mechanically, by itself,
one thing banging into another, like buffers on a shunting
goods train? I find it impossible to believe. Love, not
personal, selfish love, but Divine Love, flows always, through
everything.

Flows? Obviously, since life is always in motion. One
thing leads to another. There are processes going on, at all
times, on all scales, outside and inside us. The events,
the happenings, with their three ingredients, are something
like beads strung on the string of process. While each

happening is, in a way, complete in itself, when they are strung together the resultant 'chain of events' has shape and direction. The bee-sting I got this morning was an event, but part of the process of inspecting my hives. An election is an event, part of the process of government, a hurricane is an event in the process of the seasons.

All life consists of processes, great and small, and these processes overlap and occur side by side or within each other. Some are integrating, moving up, some are disintegrating, moving down. Some get broken and are never finished, some get bent so that their initial impulse is reversed; but all those that are completed, large or small, long or short, can be resolved into SEVEN STEPS. White light is the result of the merging of seven colours. The 'doh' of any octave has seven notes between it and the 'doh' above or below. Take any complete process you can isolate and you will find it can always be split into seven steps, the growth of a plant, the building of a house. This is the Law of Seven.

The Law of Three is relatively simple and if we look we can see it in our own lives every day. The Law of Seven is far more complex and subtle and requires a deeper insight to discern. Nevertheless these two sacred primordial laws govern the entire life of the Universe, from galaxy to atom. They underlie all science, religion and art; they penetrate into politics, economics, psychology, they are an inevitable part of the fundamental structure through which and by which all life proceeds.

I need hardly say that such profound ideas as these are not mine. They form part of the teaching of Gurdjieff of which I have spoken, the only twentieth-century man who has 'imported into life', as he expressed it, cosmological and psychological ideas encompassing everything that exists and displayed it all in a 'system' which is accessible to everyone.

We could never, it seems to me, have framed this question 'Is there anyone there?' if we were not all caught in a period of transition. We have been brought up on an aspect of eternal truth poured into a mould, the dogma of accepted religion, which no longer fits the life of our times. So the truths have become discredited because we can no longer relate the old mould to the huge body of new facts and new ideas, which seem at first sight to be at variance with what may be called the spiritual life. The transition from the Old Sacred to the New Sacred is difficult, and we haven't yet made it. The Holy Trinity has manifold associations, the Law of Three has not. It seems almost sacrilegious to call forces sacred, triads sacred, octaves sacred. They are all modern 'scientific' words and jar on the concept of holiness. It dies hard.

Yet the New Sacred is just as holy as the Old. The words do not matter. They are just the mould that shapes the new concepts. Such as we are, incomplete beings living in a world of limited dimensions, we can never understand the nature of the Prime Source. Nevertheless our understanding evolves, slowly and painfully. Our horizons expand. The scale grows vast; but, at the root of it, nothing has altered – or ever will.

To deny a Creator because He does not seem compatible with 'modern thought', is as foolish as to throw out the baby with the bathwater. We, microscopic human beings, grope our way in an *ordered* universe. At every level, laws exist, principles exist. Who made them?

Chapter 5

Where Every Prospect Pleases

I

Many years ago I was driving one hot afternoon with the Warden through one of the game reserves of Kenya. We were looking for lions; but we hadn't had any luck. Then we came to an open glade, trees on either side and a water hole down below them on our right. It was such a beautiful spot that the Warden switched off the Land-Rover and we just sat, because this is the sort of thing you come to Kenya to see. All through the glade and up the rise beyond, game were feeding. A few zebra, trim and compact, in the distance. Scraggy wildebeeste, looking undernourished, with their flat heavy horns and, in the foreground, a large herd of the delicate Thompson's gazelle. They were all cropping peacefully and swishing off the flies with their tails, lifting their heads, moving a step or two and then cropping again. It was an idyllic scene, more wonderful to me because it was strange and made me feel like a privileged intruder into the Wild, into the secret life of Nature, timeless and perfect.

The Warden put a hand on my arm, alerting me and I saw he was looking at the trees on our left. I looked too and there, out through the undergrowth, came a pride of lions. They were ambling along in a leisurely sort of way, His Majesty out ahead, stopping and looking round, sniffing the air and strolling on. Her Majesty followed, a yard or two behind, somewhat preoccupied with the kids. There were three of them, adorable, bumbling, cuddly bits of mischief, who made passes at her tail, or each other's tails, or at anything else a cub can make passes at; but who followed, dutifully enough, when she called them, as she did from time to time, to tell them to keep up.

When they first appeared, I tensed. Now, I thought, we shall see some action. For, all around them, was their food, their natural prey, within springing distance. But nothing whatever happened! That Royal Family walked right through the herd of gazelle and they hardly raised their heads! When they disappeared through the trees down to the water, I felt I had witnessed a miracle – and said so. The warden laughed. 'They know they're not feeding,' he said.

It was different later in the quick dusk when we spotted a lioness in some open ground. 'She's going to kill,' said the warden and we accelerated and made a detour out ahead of her up the slope, before we stopped and switched off. Belly to the ground, her nose working, her eyes blazing, the great cat slid by within ten feet of us, stealthily moving up wind, ignoring us as if we had not been there.

Scenes like these you do not easily forget, and when I was thinking about it the other day, I was suddenly struck by an idea which had never entered my mind before: Nature is always at peace with herself and absolutely free from sin!

It seemed obvious enough, once I had thought it; but it led me on to many things. We human beings, for instance, are part of Nature, yet we are not at peace with ourselves and certainly not free from sin. So what is our place? What is sin? And even what is Nature?

II

It is fashionable today to refer to Nature as our 'environment'. With the implication that it is subservient to us, that we can take care of it, manipulate it, plunder it or ignore it, all as it happens to suit us. We are human, of course, part of Nature; but privileged, different. And indeed we are; but not perhaps as we think we are, or as we should be.

I want to suggest another view of Nature, which may be new and strange to some of you. Organic life on earth is stretched over its surface in a thin film, as delicate as a soap bubble. A hundred degrees up or down and life, as we know it, would cease to exist. Meanwhile it teems with life. This we know; but – here is what is new – we do not think of it as having a collective life, a cosmic life, or its own. We speak of Nature in the singular, as if it was one without realizing that it *is* one, an individual, an entity with its own laws and needs and aims. Great Nature is, in fact, a Being – as you and I are beings.

We have no time to go far into this; but if you ponder on this strange idea, you will find many parallels. Great Nature has a blood circulation like us. She inhales and exhales, as we do. She constantly renews herself. She has moods, illnesses, she grows and sooner or later, like everything born into Time, she will die. And do not think of all this as romantic metaphor, but as organic fact. Just as the cells in our bodies live for a moment in a life that, by comparison, must seem everlasting to them, so we play our part for a second, in a greater life which, it seems to us, must last for ever. There are Beings on many scales. The galaxies, the sun, organic life, we, and the cells within our bodies are all living Beings. The whole Universe is alive in the glory of God!

We cannot understand the life of Beings above and below us; but at our own level, have you ever thought how the harmony and renewal of the world around us is maintained? It is so strange. Life exists at the price of death. The interlocking of nature's ecology is a miracle, but wherever we touch it, we find that something is always dying that something else may live. Eat or be eaten is a Law of God.

But there is a proviso. Every creature may kill only what it needs for its own life. Obeying this, Great Nature maintains her health and harmony and lives at peace with herself. What we call the 'beauty' of the world about us is a longing for this peace. Subconsciously also we may recognize that the price of such a peace is to be free from sin.

Sin is a man-made word. It does not exist in the natural world, which does not transgress the laws of God. 'Thou shalt not kill!' said Moses. But Nature is killing all the time! It is a strange paradox. So, since there is a good deal of talk in the world today about good and evil, right and wrong, what is it to be virtuous? What is it to sin?

III

Sin is a word you hardly ever hear today. To talk about the need to live an upright and righteous life is to invite a big switch off. Nobody cares. All such precepts seem to have become engulfed in violence, hypocrisy and greed. But the hydrogen bomb will not go away because we don't look, and to try to live a becoming and honourable life remains perfectly valid, even if the world seems to have chosen to ignore it. So, once again, what is sin?

Many able and devout men have had a great deal to say about sin. For centuries the Church has been obsessed with it. There is even a catalogue of sins with a sort of price list – how much you must pay to be absolved from different classes of sins. But there is one class which, as far as I know, is not listed and that is encroachment.

What do I mean by encroachment? Well, it takes a hundred forms. To envy, for instance, is to encroach mentally on somebody else, to wish to have what he has; to steal is a physical encroachment; to kill is the ultimate encroachment. To interfere, advise, criticize, even to be a do-gooder, is almost always an encroachment on the lives of others – and I need not point out to you that the world today is shot through with envy, greed, violence and an irresistible impulse to mind other people's business.

One result of all this is that we are moving further and further away from the world around us, the natural world of which we are a part. We are certainly encroaching on Nature. But she, because she has her own life, will sooner or later redress this imbalance. Man, who should be her chief help and strength, is sick. It is serious. If he cannot recover, our world may die.

We have the right to our place, to our need to live. No more. The moment we overstep it, we are headed for trouble. It is not murder when a cat kills a mouse: it is her right. But the cat that deliberately killed fifty mice – if you can imagine such a thing – would be encroaching, transgressing the laws of Nature. It does not happen, because Nature is

47

in harmony, in balance, in law. But plainly we are not. We encroach. We live in sin.

And where does all this get us? To dream that any of it can be changed is utopia, pie-in-the-sky. It is as it is because we are as we are, as I have often said. Meanwhile what can we do? We can struggle to see where we are going. Only by understanding can we change.

What is it that irresistibly impels us to encroach, to mind everybody else's business rather than our own? In those rare moments of remorse when we see that it is destroying us personally and collectively, we long to find another way that would lead us back to sanity and peace.

That way is not impossible to find; but it entails giving up much to which we are deeply attached.

Chapter 6

The Three Foods

I

As I sit here in my little whitewashed room, I think to myself what can I select from this world of new ideas in which I live, what can I isolate and concentrate into the pages of this book. And, as always, I find it fraught with difficulty because, before I can pass anything, I have to reach you, to touch you, find a chink in your armour, and to do that, these days, seems very very difficult.

Do you remember how the medieval alchemists asserted they could turn base metals into gold; but how they always insisted that to do this, they had to possess a certain amount of gold already? This was essential to start the process. People took them literally; but they were really speaking allegorically. For me to make gold for you, you have to have some already. That is, you have to have something to respond with, something to vibrate, something on the same wavelength, so to speak – and then we can communicate.

Now everybody has this something and can receive and transmit on these wavelengths; but because of the way life has developed in most of us, shutting us more and more into the cares and preoccupations of everyday things, this part which can respond, vibrate, come out to welcome, has been buried, mislaid; and we don't know how to reach it any more. Worse than this there is an antagonism, a repudiation, an 'I don't want to know' attitude to what is, in fact, a necessity for a healthy life. It is like someone living on a diet which has a vitamin deficiency. They become sick, without knowing why or what to do to cure themselves.

We have a good old English saying: 'You can lead a horse to water; but you can't make it drink.' And this is the first thing I have come to in this section. I can't give you anything unless you want it, without your *wish*. I can only point to the water. Whether you want to drink or not depends on something about the way I point, maybe, and the smell of the water, to which I would lead you.

We all died last night and were resurrected this morning and, after the miracle, we *could* live today as if it were our very first day on Earth! How marvellous, how new everything would be! Like childhood! How open we should be to everything. There would be no prejudices, no routines, no refusals.

I wonder if we can still make it like that? The heart of things is very simple. The more spiritual things are, the more practical they are. I would like to try to write about a simple thing, the central act of life – eating. And about the three foods we human beings eat. It's a fascinating subject.

II

Have you ever thought what keeps you going, what sustains your life? Many people's first reaction would be to say their job, their profession, their interests. But of course none of this would be possible without food. Eating is what keeps us going. Eating is a central fact of life. On what we eat and how we eat everything depends.

Today there is a great deal of interest in food. There isn't enough to go round. Some have too much, some have too little. Some waste it, some hoard it, some adulterate it, some fortify it. But food, whatever its quality, is used to maintain and renew the body's tissues, to provide us with fuel in the form of energy. Food enables us to climb mountains and break records. Food sustains life. If we don't eat, we die.

Everybody knows this; but at the same time we are told that man is a curious being. The poets, philosophers, religious teachers, all assert that man is two-natured, part-animal, part-angel, and that these two natures co-exist together in the same body, though in fact they are hardly on speaking terms, their needs are so different. Then, if we assume that food feeds the body, the animal part, what feeds the other, higher part? Can I affect my spiritual life by my diet? If I lived on caviar and strawberries would it refine my spirit? Hardly. Everybody knows instinctively almost that the food that goes in one end and out the other is necessary almost exclusively for the body alone.

Now, in general, this first food that goes into our bellies is the only food we know about or think about as food. But there are, in fact, two other foods, every bit as essential to life. We can do without 'ordinary' food, if we are put to it, for days and even weeks; but without our second food we could not live for more than two or three minutes and, if we were to be deprived of our third food, we should die at once.

Our second food is air. We take our breathing quite for granted, though it is as essential for life as our first food. But air, though it assists the refinement of our 'ordinary' food, has other purposes also. It is our second-being food. Whether we have ever thought about air as food or not, it is quite obvious that it is. We cannot live without it. But our third food is more mysterious.

It flows into us all the time in the form of what we call 'impressions'. What we see, hear, taste, touch, smell is brought to us continuously through our senses. Life itself feeds us. Our bodily and spiritual health depends directly on the sort of life to which we subject ourselves or are subjected. It is a strange idea. The highest is always connected to the lowest.

III

Let us try to take a closer look at our ordinary food. It sustains our bodies, our animal part, which we share with all the other breathing creatures on our planet. Now the whole earthly creation lives for two things and two things only – food and sex. Everything is geared to the propagation and preservation of the species and its continuation is achieved through the most wonderful and complex adaptations, so interlocked that everything, from highest to lowest, has a way of obtaining food and continuing the existence of its kind.

Man alone is two-natured and has the possibility to live beyond the body. Although his animal part is equally preoccupied with food and sex, he has other faculties, other aims, such as, for instance, the study of his own nature, which we are pursuing now.

In all growth there is a process of refinement. The lamb cropping the grass, grows into a ram with its splendid horns, its fleece, its hide. In the miraculous chemical factory of its body 'something' in the grass is refined to become something totally different. How does grass become wool and hoof and horn? It is a sort of magic.

Gurdjieff teaches that there is a primordial sacred law, the Law of Seven, governing every process in the Universe, of whatever scale. Everything is either developing or degenerating according to this sacred law. A lifetime of study could be devoted to this Law alone and I only mention it here because a striking aspect of its working is in the transformation of food, which is something close to us, our subject for study now.

You cannot have process without aim. You build a house with the aim of living in it. You make a dress to wear. The idea 'I want a house' grows into the fact 'I have a house'. The wish and the fact are reflections of one another. The word has become flesh, so to speak. Different aspects of the same creation.

When we take food into our mouths, already in the mouth the seven steps of this refining process begin. Each subsequent step is a digestion, a refining, a transformation. At each step something remains to nourish that part of the body; but the rest moves on, carried by the blood, to the stage beyond. Finally, at the seventh step, the distillate is concentrated in the ovaries of the female and the testes of the male and the self-recreation, through food taken in from the outside, can be repeated. The aim of life is the life to come.

This is the – I think, marvellous – mechanism of eating

at the animal level. But there is still the question of the human level.

IV

How do we human beings think of ourselves? In general, I would say we consider ourselves individuals with various talents and abilities, part of society, part of a changing, developing world. All our lives have a certain shape, a certain destined pattern, and the idea of changing it – even if we wanted to – seems impossible.

We certainly do not look on ourselves as chemical factories, which take in raw material, food, and turn it into energy. This is a far too mechanical, dispassionate view of life. But whether we see it this way or not, this is what is happening, all day and every day. So let us try to look at it this way for a moment.

What is important in any factory is its efficiency. How well do we transform the food we eat? Do we make use of it all? Is our machinery working as it should, as it could? Or is it just turning over, making no profit? We, as human beings, are the end-product of our factories. Are we making the best of ourselves, are we making a profit?

Gurdjieff tells us we are not. Our factories are just turning over, producing what is necessary for living; no more. The capacity of the factory is far greater. We are constructed in such a way that our potential far exceeds our present output. 'You cannot conceive', he says, 'what man is capable of attaining.'

But to increase our output changes have to be made in the way the factory works. We have to impose certain disciplines and economies in its management. In other words, if we want to profit by life, we have to live differently.

How to translate this into human terms? Suppose we admit that we are sometimes irritable, impatient, thoughtless, angry, jealous, or whatever, then it is exactly here that our factory is wasting energy. We agree, perhaps, it would be better to change this. But how? We agree we ought to impose disciplines on ourselves. But what are they? We know from experience that good resolutions lead nowhere.

Something more is necessary. There are techniques, of course; but, as I've already said, everything finally comes back to our *wish*. It is the source of all effort. It is a strange way to look at things; but if you think about it you will see that the first step to economy in our factories is to save energy. Getting angry wastes energy; keeping quiet saves it. You cannot hope for a happier life, a healthier state, if you indulge in a waste of energy.

But this is only a beginning. Tomorrow we can study the way we take in the air we breathe and the impressions that reach us. Here is the possibility of real profit.

V

We would all agree, I think, that we are two-natured. We feel there is 'something' in us which is more than the body – even if we cannot exactly define what it is. We aspire, in various ways, towards something we call a 'better' life. It is part of a subconscious wish, not understood, not focused, which tells us we could make more profit out of life than we do.

Great Nature does not require this of us. We can live quite well without it. The animals do. They are perfectly content to be what they are. A man, living as an animal, can be equally content. It is our 'other' side, the Conscience, the God in us, that summons us to develop the potential in our factories. So we do it for ourselves, for our own salvation. Nobody else is interested. If we agree to make economies, to subject ourselves to disciplines, it is to achieve this aim. It is a commitment to *work*. Just to think about it, dream about it, is useless. Fantasy.

Our biggest loss of energy comes from getting trapped into negative states. By negative states I mean our self-indulgence in various forms of egoism. Being angry does not alter a situation. Being depressed will not change the weather. Being proud will not stop other people thinking us fools. Being sorry for ourselves is a useless luxury. All these states drain us of energy. It is all waste. No factory

54

run on such lines can make a profit.

But if we succeed in resisting these traps, what does it mean? It means we have begun to cut back on our egoism, that we are not totally wrapped up in ourselves, that we see we are not the centre of the Universe. It means we have begun to stand apart from ourselves, to cut ourselves down to size.

From all this another creature begins to emerge, a man, who takes pride in not being the slave of everything about him, who begins to be master of himself. Of course he will fluctuate, be sometimes successful, sometimes not; but he will begin to see the secret is to control his fluctuations, to damp down his oscillations, to find his spine, his axis, and be steady and quiet in it.

A factory that tries to work like this has already begun to cut its losses. The manager has seen the machinery needs repair and is setting about it. It is still far from making a real profit. But a start has been made and that is something.

And you? Do you think that if you made such an effort it would not change your life? If you did it for five years, your friends would not recognize you – and, what is more important, you would not recognize yourself!

VI

I have said that this urge to live a 'better' life comes from 'something' which many call God, and I call Conscience, the Representative of the Creator within us. It is Conscience that summons us towards consciousness, the awareness of ourselves and our lives. When we begin to reach this our factories really start to make a profit.

Perhaps you do not quite understand what I mean. As you sit reading this there are things going on around you. You see the furniture, the view through the window, you hear voices maybe, birds, sounds of traffic – in a word your world is about you. But – and it's a very strange thing which we never notice till it's brought to our attention – although we know that all this is going on, in a way it isn't connected with us. It is there outside, and we are inside, and there is no active link between the two. We are cut from our source.

If you still don't follow me, try and you will very quickly see. Any time when you can be quiet and alone for a few minutes, try to be aware: 'I am here, now, looking at this room or this view or whatever.' Try to be aware both of what you see and that you are seeing it. Make the connection between the outer and inner, between your self and your world, include your world within you, merge yourself with it and yet don't lose the awareness that you are doing so.

It is more complicated to say than to do. To do it is very simple. At first when you make this effort you will find it strange. A new relation between yourself and the world about you. Here you are really looking at what you are looking at! Impressions, our third food, have been banging on the door, so to speak, all our lives and we have never allowed them to come in. Now they enter.

A moment later this delicate balance goes. Either you find you are congratulating yourself on having done it – not observing that you have already ceased to do so – or you have become interested in what you have seen or heard and lost the connection between yourself and it. In a word you can't keep it. It goes.

This is the crux of the problem. We are not living our lives: life lives itself in us – and we are disconnected from it. Like Satan, in a flash, we fall out of Heaven; that is, out of our balanced, collected state. And all our effort is to get back. The Kingdom of Heaven is within us, and we live outside it, disconnected.

The extent to which we can remain connected marks the level of our factory's efficiency. Yet, as we struggle, the whole place changes. Useless to talk about this. It has to be experienced. This is the profit our factories were designed to make. Whether they do or not, like everything else, depends on us.

Chapter 7

The Mirror

As I was going out this morning, I stopped in the hall to have a look at myself. There is a big mirror there. I examined my reflection. My suit was neat, my hair tidy, my beard was brushed, my carriage upright. Not so bad, I said to myself, not so bad for seventy-seven. And I went out into the street feeling quite pleased with myself. Or rather pleased with my appearance, my exterior, the façade I would present to the passer-by, or to my friends or those I wanted to impress.

What I saw was not my 'self', of course. It was just an image, a shell, I show to the world – and I'm quite familiar with it. It is, perhaps, the only part of myself with which I am familiar. I know what I look like.

But do I? Perhaps it would be better to say I know what I want other people to think I look like! For, after all, it is a common tendency for all of us to have a good opinion of ourselves; but it does not at all follow that others share it. We have usually no idea how awful we look or what fools we are making of ourselves. Many people during my life have, I am sure, called me arrogant, selfish, vain, ignorant, thoughtless. That wonderful impression I have of myself rarely spreads to others. In other words it is an imaginary impression. I am not what I like to think I am. The reality is different.

What is this reality made up of? It is not just the front, flat, mirror image. I am solid. I am in the round. If I could see myself from a lot of different angles, I should get quite a different impression. And this does not apply just to my exterior, it applies to my inside too. Either way, if I really want to get some idea of what I am like, I must somehow or other find a way to see myself in the round.

But do I really want to? I wonder if you ever think about

this? I know when I first started to think about it, I got a very mixed up answer. On the one hand was my complacency, my egoism, which assured me it was quite unnecessary. What I thought was right, what I did was right, my opinions, my behaviour, my attitude to life, they were all quite all right. So what was there to look at? And if, by any chance, I did find anything that wasn't so hot, well, that was me, after all. Everybody has a skeleton in their cupboard. Why rattle the bones?

On the other hand I found I was insatiably curious. I wanted to know more about this wonderful 'me' that I admired so much. If the flat reflection looked so good, the sculpture would be even more remarkable surely? Besides I had been told that every man contained hidden powers, possibilities, far exceeding his present performance. That was an attractive idea. I wanted to make the most of myself. I wanted to improve, to grow. Why not? What was life for?

And beyond all this was that irresistible magnet – Truth! Have you noticed how people cannot escape the idea of it? We all want to know the truth. We spend most of our lives trying to 'get to the bottom of things', trying to find out the truth. Usually our effort is directed towards outside things, it isn't turned in on ourselves. But the inside is the most fascinating part, after all, perhaps the last unexplored continent left to us. The question was: Did I really want to know?

Of course I didn't give any undertaking either to myself or anyone else that I would take this question I had posed seriously or carry on with it. I said to myself I would just put my toe in and see how the water was. If it turned out to be chilly, I would quickly hop out. I knew nothing about swimming in that kind of sea.

I got the idea, or rather others who were trying it warned me, that I shouldn't get very far with a looking glass. We all had, they said, another kind of mirror, an inner mirror, more like one of those instant cameras really, which would give me a snap of my behaviour, of how I was at any time – strictly private, of course, a snap of me for myself, not for my friends. And if I could build up a collection of these snaps, they said, it would give me a much better idea of myself, of how I really was.

At first it was very frustrating. I saw that I didn't really know how to go about trying to catch these images, I didn't know how to hold the camera, how to get into the shot, how to see what I saw, so to speak. It was all rather baffling. It was really, I suppose, the idea of all this that was so unfamiliar. From the occasional glimpses I got of myself, I saw clearly that I had such a mirror, that I could get new and surprising views of myself; but there was a totally unexpected snag – I almost always forgot to look! It was infuriating. I seemed to have a built-in resistance to looking at myself! It wasn't that I was scared, I wanted to see. But somehow or other I always missed out. I forgot. I found myself faced with a perfectly simple thing – and yet I couldn't do it.

That really wasn't good enough, I decided. I must narrow my sights. I would choose certain moments in the day and have a look then. I would choose, say, the moment when my wife brought me my coffee, or the moment when I first went in to see my boss. But my wife asked me a question as she came in and, in answering it, I quite forgot my intention and my boss was wearing such an outlandish tie it completely threw me and it wasn't till ten minutes later I realized that I'd absolutely forgotten my promise to myself. So I had to face it – and it was rather a come down – I simply couldn't be there to see at moments when I had definitely decided that I would be.

This forgetfulness was the first obstacle I encountered in what appeared to be a perfectly simple thing – to watch my own behaviour. I must say I found it a challenge. I could easily remember my day-to-day affairs, after all. I knew what had been said, agreed, what needed to be done, all that was easy – afterwards. But my decision to watch and see how I was *at the time*, that just didn't happen. At first I couldn't believe it. I, with all my abilities and faculties, to be beaten by something as simple as that! But there it was. I couldn't do it and I couldn't help it. On those rare occasions when I did remember, it seemed a real triumph, a red letter day.

But why get caught up in a ridiculous kind of exercise like this? I can hear you say. What is the point of all this talk about reflections, mirrors and cameras, that I have been worrying about? Why, in my opinion, is it so important that we should try to keep tabs on ourselves, learn more about ourselves and find out what we are really like, what is the nature of our personal reality? This is the crucial question. Either it seems important to you, or it does not. If it does not, then forget it. Nothing further that I have to say can be of the slightest interest to you.

For I am suggesting, of course, that all is not right with us, that we are not the wonderful people we believe ourselves to be, and that all of us, from Prime Minister to tramp, have a built-in conviction that, although we may go wrong occasionally, we are really remarkable people. Even if we subject ourselves to critical examination every now and then, it is rare for us not to end up justifying our behaviour. Indeed self-justification is the spindle upon which all our egoism is wound. But the truth is we cannot bear to look at ourselves impartially, as God might look at us, that would cut us down to such infinitesimal size, we might have no heart to go on. So we are mercifully protected from that. And yet the root of all evil and indeed what we call Evil itself, springs directly from our ignorance of our own natures and the attitudes and actions that result from it.

But isn't that a pretty sweeping condemnation? After all man *is* wonderful. He can go to the moon. He can see things hundreds of times smaller than his eyes can normally focus. He probes the galaxies, he unravels the secrets of matter, from the research laboratories of the world there pours a positive Niagara of discoveries and inventions, so vast, so varied, that computers are necessary to collate and cross-reference the information he is adding to daily. It is all extraordinary, wonderful, and we are as excited about it as a kid with a building kit. Give us another twenty years and we shall have solved the secret of life itself. Where are our shortcomings? What is all this nonsense about higher powers, about mysteries, about God? God is a back number, utterly out of date. Why bother about Him? I know. I know . . . And yet, there is something wrong.

Where has it all got us? And where is it going to get us? Don't you sometimes feel a bit apprehensive at the way things are going? The shape of things to come is a bit of a question mark, isn't it? There is something lop-sided about it. On the one hand there is this wonderful outpouring of human ingenuity, on the other hand a near breakdown in society. We have everything necessary to help us to live full, rich lives and yet daily we get more and more lost in the labyrinths of our own making.

It is the old legend of Midas. Everything he touched, you remember, turned to gold. And gold, in universal fables like this, is not just the yellow metal. It is the symbol of greed, of insane avarice, of grabbing more than you have a right to, more than you can handle or deserve. Finally, of course, the very bread that should have nourished Midas, turned to gold in his mouth and choked him. He died from his own stupidity.

Is this an exaggeration? Perhaps. But we are somehow getting desperately near it. Then is there a way out? Of course there is! But do we yet feel sick enough to go to the doctor?

Since all our unbecoming manifestations, that is, all Evil, springs directly, in my opinion, from our own shortcomings, our self-satisfaction, our complacency, our ignorance of ourselves, if we wish to find a healthier, saner life, it is to ourselves that we must come back.

I am a reflection of the Whole. In me lies the beginning, the opportunity for struggle and growth. In me lies the possibility of fulfilment. In me lies the end. Nothing can change, except I wish it. Nothing can grow, except I tend it. All possibilities, all hopes, the Godhead itself, lies within me. It is there; but I cannot find it. It whispers; but I never hear. It is within; but I always look out.

The Uni-Being Creator, the First Cause of all life, gave

me at birth – so that I might possibly be of help to Him in a growing Universe – a mirror. An inner mirror, in which I could – if I wished – begin to see myself. No other gift was necessary for me to learn everything I needed to know to fulfil all my obligations, all my responsibilities, towards myself, towards my neighbour and towards Him.

But this mirror is not like the one in my hall which just reflects a flattering façade. It is more difficult, and sometimes more bitter, to look into. Yet, if we dare to look and learn how to use it, it can reflect everything we are. For there is within us, a multitude, a world. Not only the saint but the murderer; not only the honest man but the liar; not only the generous but the mean; the dreamer, the schemer; the noble, the base; the serious, the flippant; the sage and the fool. They are all there. Only with our mirror can we see them and appraise the chaos of our state – and that, after much struggle.

But do you not think, if you were struggling to use your mirror and knew that your brother was struggling also, that you would feel a wave of compassion and pity and love for him, knowing that he could not see any more than you could, knowing that he too failed to look, forgot to look, and that you both might die blind tomorrow?

How can we help ourselves if we don't know what needs help? We need to see. We may be less than we thought we were, but we are also more. Our mirror stops us lying to ourselves and we feel clean.

And what a change such an admission of frailty could bring into our lives! For out of it can grow humility and a readiness to serve. From service grows responsibility and with that begins the birth of Conscience – which is the representative of the Creator in us. And it is the rebirth of Conscience, through our growing consciousness, that holds true objective hope for the world to come.

Turn then to your inner mirror, which, if you persist, will show you all you need to know. It is not an easy road; but as long as you tread it, you will be in a state of grace.

Chapter 8

The Kingdom of Heaven

I

As a very young man I went to China and, living in the city of Peking, I began to study the Chinese language. One day, in conversation with my teacher about Chinese literature, he told me that in Chinese poetry there were what he called 'stop' characters. These, he said, occurred like a sort of exclamation mark at some climax in the poem and had such powerful associations, so well understood by every reader, that they conjured up whole vistas of thought, illuminating everything that had gone before or was to come. When I asked him to give me examples of the sort of ideas these 'stop' characters could convey, he was unable to do so. Without an understanding of the Chinese way of thought, he said, they would have no meaning for me.

Later on I realized that, although the construction of our language is totally different from Chinese, our poets also sometimes reach moments of such incandescence that words or phrases seem to leap up from the page. These 'jewels five words long', as Tennyson expressed it, are the Western equivalent of 'stop' characters. They light up the imagination and can encapsulate the dreams of a whole generation. Some have an even deeper and longer-lasting appeal. Among them is one that seems almost eternal: The Kingdom of Heaven.

What vistas of longing and fantasy those four words have inspired! Passages in Bach and Beethoven that uplift the heart, the pure Elysian landscapes of Fra Angelico or Bellini, the wonder of the 27th Psalm, the ache in the Parables. The Kingdom of Heaven is the universal utopia of all mankind, the destiny we pray to deserve, the immortality we sigh for. It epitomizes the pathway to eternal life.

Now, although such aspirations are in every way right

and proper – and indeed our chances as human beings would
be nil if we hadn't got them – if we start seeking specific
information about this Kingdom of Heaven, it soon gets
vague and somewhat bewildering. Where and what is this
Kingdom? we ask. If we get there, what do we do? How
do we employ ourselves, make ourselves useful? Today the
artist's dream – magnificent skyscapes of cloud and sunlight
and a lot of angels floating around doing absolutely
nothing – is hard to believe. Surely Heaven must be more
than this?

Yet, although we may abandon the idea that all such
fantasies are childish and ridiculous, the idea persists that
it is somewhere all the same. Think about it. Ask yourself the question: Where and What is the Kingdom of
Heaven?

II

Do you not feel sometimes that we are all extraordinarily
naïve about the teaching of Christianity? I said the
teaching, mind, not Christianity itself. So much seems to be
taken only at surface level. We never seem to probe into
the words themselves to discover the treasure buried
beneath them.

There are different kinds of language. There is 'everyday'
language; scientific, legal, business language, which means
only what it says – if you can understand it. And there is
allegorical language – not much in vogue today – where the
words are expressly designed, not only to mean what they
say, but to cover layers and layers of meaning underneath.
This is the deep rich language of myth and of the Gospels.
And it is sad to see how, for centuries, everybody, church-
men, artists and public alike, seems to have forgotten how to
explore these hidden veins.

Take, for instance, the Nativity. It has been sentimental-
ized into little more than a beautiful fairy-tale; but, underneath, what does it mean? Who were the shepherds and
indeed who were the sheep? Why did the Wise Men come
from the East and what do their gifts mean? Then the Inn

why was there no room at it? What part do the animals play and why was the Holy Child laid in a manger? Above all, why was Jesus born of a virgin? In sacred writings, especially in the account of the birth of a new faith, it is not enough to take things literally. Deeper meanings are there, in every word, filling the mind with thought, springing out from the simple language to enrich our understanding – like those 'stop' characters I referred to before.

I seem to have strayed from the point, sharing my thoughts with you; but not so far, after all, for the Kingdom of Heaven is another apparently simple idea which is little more to us, if we are honest with ourselves, than another fairy-tale. Yet dare we afford to be so childish and woolly about something so important?

Jesus was not woolly: He was very specific. He told us to seek it *first*, and all the rest would be added to us. Well, surely that gives us a clue? It must be something to be found in this life, since there can't be much to be added after we are dead. And then He told us, absolutely clearly that the Kingdom is within us. Well, in that case, it must be some place in the present, here and now: a possibility open to us *in this life*.

The Parables are there to give us all sorts of clues. The Kingdom of Heaven is like this, or like that – yet, at the same time, it is within us. It is a riddle. But perhaps we can solve it, at least in part.

III

The Kingdom of Heaven! Let us try to take the phrase apart. To me Kingdom doesn't mean a place with geographical co-ordinates, like country or empire. It suggests more words like domain, realm – a place, but not a physical place, dominated by a king perhaps, but not a physical king. And Heaven? Well, it certainly suggests the upper atmosphere; but it also has allegorical, symbolic meanings, signifying something above us to be remembered, dreamed of and longed for.

What can fulfil all these requirements and still be within us?

First there comes an association. Peace. The Kingdom of Heaven must surely be peaceful. The very idea of war there never occurs to us. It is a place of peace. Peace and quiet. Now we are getting warmer, for peace means something to us, and quiet too. We know what the words mean. We have been peaceful. We have been quiet. We know that state.

Suppose we were voluntarily, intentionally, to pursue this idea of peace and quiet. Deliberately to look for it, 'seek it first', would that lead us towards the Kingdom of Heaven?

Certainly it would. It is the pointer to the entrance, the way in. But remember that the Kingdom is a pearl of great price. It is not to be had for nothing. All we have to pay with is our *wish*, our longing, to get there. And, alas, most of us haven't a strong enough wish to buy a seed pearl.

But let us suppose we really wish to pay, then we can begin seriously to try to quieten ourselves, seriously to struggle for our inner peace. How? By shutting out the conflict, the war in our heads which continually, exasperatingly, from morning till night, comes between us and our wish for peace. Arguments, explanations, contradictions, justifications, all of them imaginary, like spectres or ogres, endlessly at war with one another and with our longing for quiet.

All these have no place in the Kingdom of Heaven. They are insolent intruders; but we have to fight to drive them out. That is how we pay. There are ways to rob them of their strength, weapons with which to wage this inner war, people to help. My part is simply to awake in you the idea, the possibility. 'Seek and ye shall find. Knock and it shall be opened unto you.' Not in some woolly never-never land; but here and now, in this life. For quiet is something we can find anywhere, once we make room for it. Quiet in our sitting, quiet in our walking, quiet in our thought. And as we begin to get the taste of this state, the longing for it grows in us. And, if we persevere, fighting our way back to it again and again, we may at last reach something marvelous – being never so apart from life and yet never so deeply in it, never so empty, yet never so full. We are there or a second and fall back into chaos. But, if we have reached t once, we can reach it again. There is more beyond, believe me; but this is the threshold of the Kingdom of Heaven.

Chapter 9

The Power of Choice

I

Pretty well every morning as I listen to the News, I am
almost overwhelmed by the miserable state the world seems
to be in. Strikes, kidnappings, *coups*, wars and rumours of
wars, it seems as if the whole planet has been infected by
some virus, some terrible epidemic, which impels us all,
in various ways, to destroy everything, to intimidate, coerce,
humiliate and murder to get what we think we want, what
we imagine will improve our situation or achieve our
security – as if there is, or ever has been, any such thing as
security!

And as we sigh or shake our heads at what seems to be a
universal madness, two thoughts come uppermost in our
minds: first, that we can't do anything about it; second, that
we, personally, are quite free of such sub-human impulses.
We don't want to fight anyone or destroy anyone, all we
want is to be left alone to live at peace with our neighbour.
It seems to me that these are the general reactions to this
situation, which hangs like a thunderhead above our lives.

But are they true reactions? What should I do if somebody attempted the rape of my wife? I take an extreme case
to test myself and I confess I find myself full of contradictory
motives. I call myself peaceful; but I could not trust myself
in an emergency. There are all sorts of people inside me:
'My name is legion, for I am many.' And as to the other
question, is it true that we, the little people, the silent
majority, is it true we can do nothing about it?

When we set up questions like this which really confront
us with our own inner nature on the one hand and the nature
of our attitude to life on the other, it must be plain to us
all that there are no easy answers and certainly no quick
or simple ones. But we all want simple answers and the more
complex life gets, the more we hanker for simplicity.

68

And, of course, at the end the answers are perfectly simple. 'Serve God and keep His Commandments, for this is the whole duty of man.' But that isn't at all easy, for I find in the coming and going of daily life, I don't really know *how* to serve Him and have only a vague idea of *how* to apply His Commandments to everyday events. Or take that even more appealing exhortation 'Cast thy burden upon the Lord.' Have you ever tried to do it? I have, and I soon found that to let go, absolutely to give up my personal life, was quite beyond me, I didn't know how.

The road to simplicity was always obstructed by 'how'. It is this 'how' that excites and calls me, for I long ago became convinced that without a method, a discipline, a technique, if you like, it was pretty well impossible to get anywhere.

How to deepen my understanding is, to me, the ultimate question in life. But *how* to set about it?

II

Along this road towards simplicity, which we all I think, consciously or subconsciously, long for, are many obstacles – and also many pointers. One of them, both obstacle and signpost, is what we call 'influences'. We are all bombarded day and night by various influences. We are influenced by those nearest to us, by our health, the weather or our colleagues. We are influenced by the mass media, by world events and not least by that conglomerate of memories we call experience. We are, in fact, complex tape recorders, in which everything that happens to us is stored.

All this we cannot escape – even though we don't remember a hundredth part of it. But we have been endowed with a faculty which differentiates – or can differentiate – between the things we remember and those we discard. *We can choose.* We can stand, so to speak, at the front door of our house and allow some influences to enter and refuse others. It is a much more important faculty than it appears at first sight. The way we live our lives depends to a very large extent on the influences under which we

live it. And we can deliberately, that is consciously, choose
the influences. But, in general, we don't.

This daily bombardment under which we live is so complex that it doesn't seem possible, until we begin to think
about it, that it can be divided into influences of different
kinds. But there are in fact three categories, three qualities,
of influences, all of which play, or can play, their part in
our lives.

The first of these are Sacred Influences, what we call
religious influences. They come from outside 'ordinary'
life and mix with it. They become diluted and lost and so
are brought back to us, from age to age, by the teaching
of enlightened beings who may be called Sacred Messengers.
They come to remind us, if we can listen, of the possibility
of another kind of life, to which we may aspire, even
though we cannot reach it. Not many people today choose
to put themselves wholly under this group of influences.

The second category form a link between higher and
lower influences and I shall say something about them
later on. Meanwhile, what may be called 'lower' influences
need little explanation. They are the mundane everyday
happenings of life and they fill 99% of our days. They have
become so maddeningly attractive today that because we
are easily persuaded, easily suggested to, they hypnotize
and terrify us, seduce and intimidate us until our whole
lives are lived under their domination. How splendid the
new car! How dreadful the latest bomb! How gay the new
clothes! How crippling the new taxes! News, sport, sex,
food, money, these are the things that in varying degrees
according to our temperaments, fill our days to the exclusion of everything else. These are the materialistic influences
to which we are all too ready to succumb. This is, in a way,
the armour we put on to protect us against God.

III

Between the influences of everyday life and those higher
influences that have their origin outside it, lie another
category which strive to interpret or reconcile the two.

It is said that, once upon a time, in the Golden Age, a great University existed in which groups of people who had, by their own pondering and struggling, understood some aspect of Truth, created various means of expressing it, in order to transmit it to later generations. These were the first artists and this was the original intention and purpose of art. Pure truth could be too abstract, too deep, to be reached; but an aspect of it, enclosed in some artefact, like a bee in amber, could become accessible, appealing, and so open us to feelings which had hitherto remained dormant in us. The artists hid these truths in sculpture, in architecture, in paintings, in music, in ritual, in the theatre, calculating that their effect would be to arouse our sleepy souls to seek out what they meant.

A few of these works of art, or their true derivatives, still exist today. There is, for instance, a seated Chinese figure in the British Museum, which embodies the very essence of meditation. What is the truth hidden behind that steadfast calm? There is a church in Meteora built in such proportion that as soon as you enter it, you are seized with an irresistible impulse to pray. But what is prayer, and what can I understand through it? There is the lonely majesty of the Great Pyramid, the All of its apex proliferating to the Everything of its base. What is it saying? The descent of the Creation? The ascent of Man? I don't know. But I ponder. I wonder. I seek.

These man-made creations were once a third kind of influence, a sort of link, a jumping-off place for the spirit. Today they have turned into their own opposite, an amusement, a titillation, a status symbol or an investment. The high purpose has gone – but it could be reborn.

Meanwhile here we are, sandwiched between the Stock Market and the News Bulletin. In a moment we shall be beseiged by the clamour of the everyday world. It is rather like a trip on a dodgem – being banged into by everybody around us. Hilarious for ten minutes, but hardly a pattern for life! But we cannot escape it. We are not meant to. Precisely here is the material for struggle. For we can choose the influences under which to live. We need not be

flattened out, run over, by life. We can get up. We have
other instincts which can lead us to seek an inner harmony –
always balanced precariously between our two worlds.
That is where we were born to stand. It is an indictment
and a challenge for Man to call himself the Crown of
the Creation. Which of us, today, is fit to wear one? Well
– I leave it to you . . .

Chapter. 10

Good and Evil

I

You have to be outside it to see it, don't you? If I say 'This is good', then I must be separate from it, looking at it. If I say 'This is bad', then it is some other part of myself that condemns it. We all have a sort of code by which we divide the valuable and worthless, the beneficial and harmful, the right and wrong. At some point we, so to speak, insert a knife into life. The patient, kindly, tolerant man divides it so that almost everything is 'good'. The violent, embittered, revengeful man so that it is almost all 'evil'. How do either of them choose?

However they choose, it is obviously a personal matter. It is *their* point of view, their opinion. Pirandello once wrote a play which he called *And that's the truth – if you think it is*. In it he showed a group of people, each with his own idea of what had happened in a certain situation. As the play developed the truth kept changing; but each of the characters continued to think they were 'right'. The right and the wrong, the good and the evil, were individual. There could be no final decision that satisfied everybody.

Of course there are generalities on which our code of opinions is based. Some of them are quite ephemeral. Fashion, public opinion, what is 'done' or not done, these are responsible for quite a lot of what we call good or bad, right or wrong. There is also a very large complex of judgements, called laws, which lay down social justice. Behind all this lies a set of principles, often called commandments, which make basic statements: 'Thou shalt not kill', 'Thou shalt love thy neighbour as thyself.' But these do not seem to come from the same source as the man-made laws. It is as if there were two codes of good and evil, a god-made code and a man-made code. They are not the same. One is changeless, the other varies from country to country, from generation to generation.

In England at one time a man could be hanged for stealing a sheep – or, at best, exiled to Australia. In some countries a man may discard his wife simply by saying three times 'I divorce you'. That would hardly be sufficient to obtain a decree in a Western community.

In the course of our lives all these commandments, laws and conventions have been absorbed by each of us. They are often contradictory, and so there results a sort of personal 'hotchpotch' concerning good and evil, right or wrong. On the basis of this hotchpotch, we are ready to judge, condemn, affront and even murder our neighbour, if he fails to agree with us.

It is quite a muddle and, if we are honest with ourselves, it isn't at all easy to decide what is good and what is evil.

II

Although you may agree that good and evil are always related to us and that each of us holds different points of view about them, it is surely undeniable, as we look around the world today, that we see a good deal of what, in general, we should call 'evil'. We see mass murder, the abuse of power, social corruption, anarchy, the callous disregard of suffering – all on a global scale, so widespread, so endless, we cannot really take it in. In contrast, our personal lives seem innocent, simple, blameless in comparison. Yet we appear to be caught up in a whirlwind of forces we can in no way resist or control. We are frustrated and conclude by shrugging it all off. It is too big for us.

That may, in part, be true. Though it doesn't help in the long run, there is a theory that our planet – and indeed the whole solar system – is at present passing through a noxious part of space and being subjected to influences which disturb what we might call our psychological metabolism and predisposes the entire human race to a highly charged emotional state, a global attack of the jitters. After all, it has been better, or at any rate a good deal quieter, in days gone by. There was even, it is rumoured, a Golden Age, in which evil did not exist. How to explain these cycles of change except by the action of some quite extraneous 'atmosphere' which causes these fluctuations in behaviour?

Whether all this is true or not – and it would certainly be difficult to prove it – it is also undeniable that coupled with, and even in proportion to, this tidal wave of 'evil', there is an opposing force or tendency, all over the world, which seems to incite people to look for something different, something better, something to rescue them from this state of affairs which they can in no way prevent, but want no part in.

It is as if this noxious area acted on us all as a strange sort of stimulus; producing in some an urge to destroy, in others an urge to create, or recreate, a more tolerant and sane existence for all of us.

But when we have finished putting the blame on some hypothesis like this, we have, alas, to come back to the fact that societies are aggregates of individuals. Our collective longings are, finally, personal longings. It all comes back to rest on the feeble shoulders of you and me.

We are like magnets. One end fears, despairs, destroys, the other longs, hopes, believes in some 'better' life. Suspend the magnet and it points – and always in the same direction – held in the field of force of our eternal destiny.

III

If we can agree that God and Satan, good and evil, are an integral part of the make-up of every human creature, it leads us to a very awkward question. If some Great Originator, some force we call 'God', created the Universe, then He must have created everything within it – including Satan. In fact there is a famous passage in the Scriptures: 'And I saw Satan falling like lightning out of Heaven.' Out of Heaven. But 'Heaven' is the traditional abode of God, so Satan must be, or must have been, one of God's helpers, a special angel perhaps, whose destiny was to confront mankind with all those difficulties we call 'evil'. He was not banished from Heaven. He simply fell in a magnificent flash of fire, to be the tormentor, the eternal discord, in the human soul. Part of God then, and part of life. But why? To what end?

If you want to be an athlete, you must diet, exercise, subject yourself to a strenuous routine. It is an effort you make towards an aim you have set yourself. It involves a struggle between letting go and holding on. There is always the temptation to give up, always the incentive to excel. It seems that this desire to attain a goal is a basic fact of life, built in to every human creature. All life continually struggles to recreate itself. Many creatures die as soon as they have attained it. Their struggle is against another set of forces which combine, with astonishing ingenuity, to destroy those who wish to create. It is an extraordinary paradox. Life continues only under an endless threat of extinction!

We are all caught in this dilemma. What is true for Nature, is also true for us. We are part of Nature and can also recreate ourselves. But for some reason, we have been given a further opportunity, the possibility of creating within ourselves another part, another body, which we see as the abode of our spiritual life and in which lies the hope of our immortality. The struggle to create this, though it is different, is every bit as great as any struggle in the 'natural' world.

So we come to see that, at any level, Satan is our good angel. He is our spur to struggle, the friction maker, the father of fighters. He provides the fence I have to jump, the dragon I have to slay. Victory means life: defeat means death. And the whole situation placed there before me, created by the Divine Will of God! What an extraordinary situation!

IV

This inner mechanism by which we divide everyday events into good and evil, right and wrong, is not fixed, changeless, static. It continually fluctuates. A man calls me a fool, and immediately my opinion of him veers towards the 'evil' side. He is 'bad'. But the next day he does me an unexpected kindness and I am obliged to revise the estimate. He is not so bad after all. It is the same with everything, from the political situation to the colour of my tie, my like or dislike of them varies with the weather, the time of day, my health, whether I have had a drink or not, what the papers say, and so on. My inner barometer of good and evil always stands at 'Change'.

The realm of Satan lies in this world of change. He works among the variations and vacillations in which we all live. He is king of the weathercocks. He uses this no-man's land between right and wrong, yes and no, to perplex and confound us. Right is wrong. Good is bad. I hate what I love and love what I hate. There is no end to the confusion he creates within us. Yet when we have given up, settled for taking the easy way out, there remains another part which subtly, stubbornly, continues to struggle against what we sometimes call our 'lower nature' and fights – sometimes successfully, sometimes not – to find a steadier, more impartial viewpoint – a 'good' place where I am more free from the hurly-burly which deafens and distracts me.

It may help if I try to give you a picture of the human being you will not find in books on psychology. The part of us that is constantly changing we may call the personality: the part that is more constant we may call the soul. Our personality is rather like a man with a big wardrobe. He always dresses to suit his company. He has, for instance, a suit he always wears with his wife. Another he always wears with his children, another for his boss, his cronies, his mistress. He can change with lightning rapidity from suit to suit; but he cannot wear two suits at once. While he is angry, he is *all* anger; when he is affectionate, he is all affection. Try to watch yourself any day, any time and you will see that it is so. Where is the liar, when the lover is present? Where is the lover, when the wife turns up? There is nothing permanent about us, such as we are. We are legion. Very many.

A man builds up his wardrobe in youth. Thereafter he must always wear the same suits. He cannot discard them. He cannot go about naked. Yet they are not him. He is not his suits. Suits may wear out; but they are not alive. They cannot grow; but the man is alive and can grow. He may grow so that some of his suits don't fit him and he cannot wear them any more.

Our struggle between good and evil is the struggle to reduce the size of our wardrobe. It may happen that, at last, a man has only one suit which he never changes. Then he is a saint.

V

We spoke of the knife we could insert into life to divide what we call 'good', from what we call 'evil'. What is this knife? How, in different situations, can we cut life in two?

It is very simple. The knife is my aim. Whatever leads me towards my aim, I can call good; whatever leads me away from it, I can call evil. *My* aim need not necessarily be good from anybody's point of view but my own. The man who succeeds in blowing up an airliner, and himself as well, has carried out an aim which to him – since he was prepared to die for it – must have seemed good. To the rest of us it may seem exceedingly evil. I have taken an extreme case; but, in general, we must see that good and evil have no meaning except in relation to the aim in view. 'Heaven' and 'Hell' only exist in relation to that.

Some people are lucky enough to have an aim that remains constant. They have always wanted to be a millionaire or a general or a painter. They are lucky. To have an aim simplifies life. If we want a thing constantly, to the exclusion of everything else, we can usually get it.

But most of us have no aim. We are not going anywhere. We drift. We take what turns up. So our lives are just a series of accidents. What 'happens'. We take what comes and hope to get by. We are quite passive to life. If we live like this – and most of us do – we can have no yardstick, no discrimination, to measure either good or evil. 'Satan finds work for idle hands to do', says the old proverb. In respect of aim, most of us are idle and sometimes when we wake up to it, we do see that our life is hell.

To live without an aim is to live without a compass. I may not reach my goal, but at least I can point towards it. Aim is very simple, yet very difficult. For, if I ask myself – and I should ask myself daily – 'What do I want – now?', it is not an easy question to answer.

Yet, once we have seen the need for aim and the value of it, aim can be trained. It can grow in us. Usually we set ourselves aims far too big for our powers – and far too vague. So we fail to carry them out and become discouraged. The way to train ourselves in aim is to have a small one, but *carry it through*. This is what is important.

A man may have a long-term aim to be a millionaire; but he must start by saving a penny a day. If he does this, he gains confidence and strength. He has established a principle. If he just dreams of wealth, as most of us do, he is unlikely to get it.

So this is another aspect of good and evil. It is an active or passive attitude to life. Aim is the search for something we value. In struggling towards it, we fight our passive side, our evil genius and reach towards the active, the creative, which is Divine.

VI

If you have come this far with me and agree that good and evil are not independent abstractions outside us, but exist only in relation to me, inside me, then, if evil is the drifting, vacillating, passive side of our lives, what is the good side?

The Devil is, on the whole, so much nearer to us – and

so interesting – that we spend most of our lives trying to deal with him. Our evil genius fascinates us: good is rather a bore. Yet Satan, as we saw at the beginning, is one of the angels, an aspect of God. So perhaps we turn so constantly towards him because we can legitimately love him and should do, since he is part of the Divine and provides us with our opportunities for struggle.

But what of the other aspects? What of the 'good' aspect which we see as set against the evil. It is more difficult to define. I don't know how it is with you; but, for my part, I find that although I spend most of my life in a sort of no-man's land of dreams and doubts, longing for this, imagining that, hoping in this possibility, deciding on that line of action – and then changing my mind, I find that, every so often, I come back to something different, something that I really want, and this 'something' is what I call 'good'.

It seems that we do not look on good and evil equally, dispassionately. If you ask yourself would you rather be a 'miserable sinner' or a saint, I fancy that, almost without thinking about it, you would plump for the saint. Why? Of course there is the weight of the way we have been brought up and live. We are all so used to the idea that however much we may fall short, good is 'better' than evil, we hardly stop to question it. But all the same it remains a valid question.

It seems that there exists in every man, however deeply it may be covered, a part of him which can be touched. He continually fluctuates – we all do – but every so often, he glimpses the chance of another way of life, of behaviour which would simplify things, free him from the complications and frustrations of everyday life. It may only be another dream; but it is a powerful one and calls him in an extraordinary way. It is a state he longs for where he can 'put down his heavy load'.

It is in fact the great involuntary and evolutionary forces at work in him. Everything proceeds from the One to the many, proliferates into the multitude and each particle of the multitude for ever strains back towards the One. The struggle permeates everything. Call it good and evil,

God and Satan, life and death, it is a primordial law of the Universe.

Everything pulls me down; everything urges me up. I stand at the crossroads. At every moment I can die. At every moment I can renew my life. I am impaled on this cross of choice. It is one of the deep meanings of the Crucifixion.

Chapter 11

Meditation

I

Meditation is a word in common use today. But what is meditation? What does it mean to 'meditate'? Is it valuable? Do I need it? Can it help?

My dictionary defines the word as 'to think deeply'. That sounds fair enough. But when we try it, what happens? Suppose we want to solve some serious problem. We take ourselves off on our own to 'think' about it. I don't know how it is with you; but, for myself, whenever I try this, I find that within seconds, I am off at a tangent, thinking about something else, often something quite trivial or irrelevant. When I notice this and bring my attention back to my problem, I find that fatally, within a very short time, I am off again! There is something very simple and very strange about meditation – which we don't really like to face up to – try as we may, the process of 'thinking deeply' evades us – we can't concentrate, as we say; we simply *can't do it.*

Why? The answer lies in our failure to recognize something basic about the human mechanism. Such as we are, in our ordinary state, we do not *think* at all. We only associate. Association passes for thinking. We have, in fact, a very extraordinary mechanism in our heads which exists to do precisely this – and cannot do anything else. It is a sort of highly complex card index which, when we feed it an idea, or even a word or a smell, at once throws up everything which, from past experience, we associate with this idea or word or smell.

Each of these associated ideas is, in turn, linked to other ideas and these again lead on to still other ideas. So, in the course of seconds having, say, a problem connected with my wife's illness, I find I am riding a donkey in North China. People often feel guilty about this. They think they ought o be able to concentrate. But we can't escape the mechan-sm. *We are like that.*

This card index is, in fact, the seat of personality. People are judged brilliant or foolish simply by the way they are able to use the material they can pull out from their inner 'files'. Besides this, we all learn in the course of life to use this mechanism in our own particular way. We make, as it were, paths through it. We acquire 'patterns' of thought-patterns, that is, of associations.

None of this is thinking. There is nothing *new* in the card index. It is all old stuff, on file. To think is to discover something new. These tapes on which all our experience is recorded, lie on the ground floor, so to speak, of our heads. To think we have to go upstairs. But this requires effort, as it is easier to pull out something from the card index — it sounds almost as good.

This is how we get stuck with ourselves. All the same, if we want it enough, we can learn how to 'think deeply', how to meditate.

II

This card index in our heads is really an extraordinary box of tricks. It is absolutely essential for everyday life. Where would we be if we could not associate, could not find our material, if we had no memory? Yet, as far as our inner life is concerned, it is a terrible obstruction. It is always in our way.

Nearly all our associations give rise to opinions about things, points of view. Facts are rare. Indeed, outside mathe-matics, it is doubtful if there are many facts. It has been said that all prayers boil down to: 'Lord, please make it so that twice two is not four.' We want things to be other than they are. Nearly all our lives are devoted to realizing some dream or another. When these dreams begin to blow up in our faces, as they are very apt to do today, then, in our dis-illusion, we say: There must be some reason why things never seem to turn out as we think they will. But how can we reconcile ourselves to this? There must be a 'real' world.

But where is it? How can we reach it? For although what we are seeking is hard to define, we instinctively believe would help to sort us out – if we could find it.

But it isn't easy and we begin to be dismayed when we find ourselves going round and round, trapped in the associative mechanism in our heads. It is then perhaps we begin to long to free ourselves from our evil genius – for evil is most of the time – and find our way to something deeper on which to rest.

But how? That is the problem. Teachers, in all religions have devoted a lot of attention to this. They tell us that the first step is somehow to stop the waste of energy that pours out of us in so called 'normal' life. But again, how?

We have to get hold of the difficult idea that *we* do not think. The mechanism functions everlastingly inside me. *It thinks in me.* It has used up a great deal of my energy and it is in my interest to stop it. But I can't stop this dynamo of turning thoughts. If I try – as I have been told to 'make my mind a blank', it simply doesn't work. I can't 'stop' thought. I shout Stop! – and it all goes on just the same.

So I have to be more intelligent, more subtle. I must find some trick by which to divert this flow of energy into another channel. The trick is hard for some people, but it is simple just to try to begin to be quiet inside. It isn't perhaps until we try, we see the 'rush hour' inside our heads. Seeing that can be the birth of longing, a yearning, to be still.

III

To see that we really have a need for quiet in our lives is a big step, much bigger than we think. Most people do not like quiet – they are frightened of silence. It is common to say we want 'to get away from it all'; but that usually only means substituting a crowded bathing beach for a crowded city. Quiet is a very different thing and although, later on a man can be quiet anywhere, it is better to begin by accepting our own limitations. We must start from where we are – ordinary, simple people, redeemed by seeing a need for

omething else. Something we can neither clearly formulate
or understand.

To see our need is a very big thing. To realize it is a
igger. For we have to take positive action, every day, to
ry to withdraw from our daily round, to retreat from life.
f I really want to be quiet, I have to make a place for it.
And here I come to the first test of my sincerity. Do I really
want it? If I do, I can always make time for it – if not, there
re a million excuses – I never wake early enough, my family
interrupts me, I shall miss my train, I have an urgent prob-
em that preoccupies me, and so on.

Of course bringing something new into our lives like this
n't easy. We are bound to fail. But it may be we notice
that the days on which we fail don't go so well and this may
ring us back to the need we felt at the outset when we
egan. If we just drift into the idea of being quiet, we shall
rift out again. It is necessary to have a moment of decision.
give an undertaking to myself. *I will do this.* I will even
ry to make it a habit, like washing my face or combing
my hair. If I can get it into my body like this, my body
will help me.

So I decide to be quiet. But what does it mean: quiet?
f I just sit and stare into space, I shall be off in a daydream
within thirty seconds. If I try to think about something, it
will be the same. Here I am, wanting to be quiet – and I
on't know how!

Every aim has a technique. To get to the moon requires
technique, to play a good game of golf or to make a pot
f jam, needs knowhow. The aim to be quiet is no exception.
need a technique to help me.

I have only time to tell you the first and most important
art of this technique today. It lies in posture. The outside
reflects the inside. Our way of standing, walking, sitting,
shows how we are. A man with a hurried walk, is hurrying
inside – a man flopped in an easy chair is slouching inside.
Quietness is not to flop, to give up. So first, I sit up. My
spine is erect. I carry my head well. I am intensely alert –
but I do not move. I am active, not passive. This is the
first thing. I am holding on, not letting go.

IV

When we manage to reach these moments of quietnes:
all the cares and preoccupations of life drop away. The
have no place here, no importance. But we cannot com
mand them and there often come periods of dismay whe
all the struggle seems useless. It must be so. The growth o
the inner life is not linear. There are periods of stagnatio:
when we cannot work at all, and then, suddenly, we seer
to jump to a new discovery.

These discoveries are often to see the connection betwee
things. They are milestones on the road towards the unit
of everything that exists. They are usually unexpected
but it is impossible to mistake these thoughts that leap
fullgrown, into the mind, for the ordinary associativ
mechanism. They have quite a different quality. When the
come to people, by luck, as they sometimes do, they ar
called moments of inspiration, of genius – but it is, in fac
only another part of the head working, a better part, a par
that thinks, and we are so unused to thought, it seems
revelation.

Such a result is not something to work for. In fact w
should not, and indeed cannot, work for results. The sudde:
thought surprises us – but we may see how it is connecte
with other moments that have gone before. It is as if ther
were another life going on above the ceiling of the room w
live in and chinks of light sometimes shine, for a moment
down through its floor.

But now, rather late, a question has come into my head
We have been talking about the merits of meditation
without ever having asked the first question: why do w
want to meditate at all? Is it just to escape the hurly-burl
of life, to be quiet, and occasionally, to 'see' things? Hav
we struggled on for months and years – for quiet is certainl
not something you can reach overnight – for no more tha:
this? Surely not?

I do not think it is possible for anyone to come to :
discipline like this unless, over the years, some dissatisfac

ion has grown up at our lives as they are. We look for
ways to reconcile ourselves to this feeling that we are not
s we should be and we seize on the idea of meditation with
feeling that it will help us to reach the heart of the matter.
And indeed it will. The heart of the matter is to see our-
elves, our way with our neighbours and the sense and aim
f this life. Such things are only possible if we are very quiet.

V

This wonderful work of meditation, once we have made
place for it, does indeed root and grow in us, brimming over
nto daily life and bringing a new attitude to everything
nd everyone about us. It is as if we had reorientated our
fe and were beginning to find a new centre of gravity.

Such an adventure is often spoken about as a journey, a
movement in time. *Pilgrim's Progress* and many other similar
ecords see it as an allegory in these terms. But, in fact,
here is no journey. We are not going anywhere. We are
here already. We have only to find ourselves in the place
here we are.

So we try patiently to hold the question: 'Who am I?'
nd every small grain of new understanding that comes in
editation opens, widens, deepens the sense of reality –
OW. We begin to see we are not what we thought we
ere. In a way we are less; in a way we are more. We begin
find in ourselves another quality of being. There is,
fter all, something real beneath the fancy dress we have
lways been wearing. Of course, we do not let this work
e seen. It is our secret. With others we continue to wear
ur fancy dress, to play our dream role. It is what they
xpect. We keep up the illusion. Not to do so would be to
npose ourselves on those to whom such work would have
o meaning.

There is nothing new about all this. Everything has been
nown about it for centuries – yet it always seems new to
veryone who discovers it. Hear how the Emperor Marcus
Aurelius spoke about it all those hundreds of years ago:
'Men seek out retreats for themselves, cottages in the

country, lonely seashores and mountains. Thou too a
disposed to hanker after such things: and yet all this is th
very commonest stupidity; for it is in thy power, wheneve
thou wilt, to retire into thyself: and nowhere is there ar
place whereto a man may retire quieter and more free fror
politics than his own soul; above all if he have within hir
thoughts such as he only need regard attentively to be a
perfect ease: and that ease is nothing else than a we
ordered mind. Constantly then use this retreat, and rene
thyself therein: and be thy principles brief and elementar
which, as soon as ever thou recur to them, will suffice t
wash thy soul entirely clean, and send thee back withor
vexation to whatsoever awaiteth thee.'

VI

We set out to explore the idea of meditation and we hav
discovered there are a lot of problems connected with i
We don't seem to have got very far. Or have we? Let u
recap.

First we examined the everyday mechanism in our head
and saw how it was geared not to concentration, but t
dispersion. We began to realize how immensely powerfu
these forces are – the forces that keep us where we are. The
came the suggestion that if we could somehow depriv
them of their power, we might be able to control then
A possible way to do this was to see for ourselves th
monster that lives our lives for us. Then came the idea tha
quietness was not just relaxation, letting go – but was, i
fact, a desperate holding on to the peace we were fightin
our way to. Lastly there was the important point that ou
struggle to find quiet would be greatly helped by ou
posture.

It may not sound much, but, believe me, anyone who ha
seen as much as this has come a long way, has begun, i
fact, to live a new life. But there is still a long way to go

So here I sit. I am composed and alert, erect and quie
watching my thoughts like a cat, trying desperately not t
let them slip off like lizards into all sorts of nonsense. Bu

I have to confess, I can't do it. In a moment I shall be lost again in my dreams. But then I have an idea. It is a trick, really. If I could give my head something to do, that might tether it, control it, make it my servant not my master. I mustn't leave a vacuum. Nature abhors it. I must occupy my mind, give it something, not perhaps what it wants to do, but what it can do. The odds are against me, of course. The weak, struggling part that wants something different has been, all our lives, at the mercy of this demon in our heads.

How many legends and fairy-tales there are about this! Jack and the Beanstalk, David and Goliath, St George and the Dragon. They all say the same thing. There is a monster to be subdued and the monster is inside me, right in our heads! Make no mistake, it is a terrible adversary. It comes on like a lion, slides away like a snake, flies like a bird, dives like a fish. No phantom has more disguises.

But I have my bait, my trick: I give it something to do. I invite it, for instance, to count, 1, 100; 2, 99; 3, 98, and so on. I suggest it watch my breathing – without altering it – I give it a short prayer to repeat 'Lord have mercy upon me', or I take it on a tour of my body, inviting it to watch over the relaxing of my limbs, one by one, in turn. It works. With such things I can tether my mind.

Now I begin to be really quiet, full of power and perfectly still. I do not move. It would break my state. How long can I keep it?

Chapter 12

Good Resolutions ·

I

Do you ever make 'good resolutions'? I confess I used to;
but I long ago gave it up, because I found it was really
impossible to keep them. So what was the use?

All the same the *idea* of good resolutions gives us a sort
of starting point and, in the crazy mixed-up world of today
it seems to me that what we all need, in our struggles to try
to cope, is a new starting point.

The fact is that we are all punch-drunk from the assault
of the mass media. We are bombarded all day and night by
TV, radio and the newspapers. We are told far too much,
worried far too much, frightened far too much, and the
effect of all this is to make us insensitive, callous, indifferent,
to everything. Our hearts and minds are really bruised by
all this information. We can't feel anything any more, except
a sort of frustrated guilt – and, of course, we can't do anything about it.

On the other hand, when we look around at our friends
and relations, our colleagues and acquaintances, we see
that they are, on the whole, reasonably decent people.
Men and women, individually, seem quite all right; but
collectively, when they get caught in the web of some cause
or some great idea, it really does seem like a virus, an
epidemic, to which they have to succumb. And the very
difference between the comparative sanity of our personal
lives and the madness of the world at large is, in itself, a
dreadful contradiction.

So, since we can't see any way out, because it is all
'beyond us' as we say, we live in a state of deep frustration
and disillusion. Everything gets more and more difficult
and hopeless. Why make any effort, why make any plan,
above all why make any 'good resolutions', since everything
is sure to be wrecked somehow. I don't think this is an

exaggeration of the state of affairs. It is, humanly speaking, a desperate situation for us all. And, over and above all this, we know that some maniac has only to press a few buttons to blow our whole civilization to bits! How on earth have men and women allowed themselves to get caught up into such a madness?

Somehow, some day, the world has got to come through all this. It is like a man on a precipice. Either he commits suicide by jumping over or he struggles back away from it, appalled by the state he must have been in even to think of it.

To struggle back from the brink, which is what we all hope must happen, the prospective suicide must have seen something about his situation, his frenzy, his madness. Something must have overcome it, have been more powerful than his folly. He must have 'come to himself', saved himself by his resolution, surely a good resolution?

So we are back where we started: everything starts with some sort of decision or resolution; but what should ours be?

II

Let us continue to ponder this idea of good resolutions, of 'making up our minds' as we say, to 'do' something, to behave in some better way which will help us or those about us. If we have seen that something of this kind is possible, it must be because one part of us has passed judgement on some other part and has come to the conclusion it would be better if we could stop this or change that. When we reach that point two things have happened: first, we have noticed something about ourselves; second, we have begun to wish to find some direction away from our present situation towards another state which would be more desirable or useful to us.

Now these are two very important things; basic things which, if we really followed them up, could radically change our lives. This ability to examine ourselves, to criticize ourselves, is something essentially human. A cow does not make a good resolution to be a better cow, or an apple tree resolve next season to yield bigger and sweeter apples. Only human beings are blessed and cursed with this ability to recognize they are *not what they should be* – and could be different. It is this ability to aspire, the 'divine discontent' of the poets, that sets us apart from the rest of the creation. It is a privilege, a possibility, a challenge and, at the same time a responsibility, a burden, a cross. For, finally, it means that our whole life becomes a question. Nothing is certain, nothing is guaranteed. We have been given life, that is all; pushed in off the deep end and left to sink or swim. Thereafter our whole problem, both in a perfectly practical way and in a more subtle 'inner' way, is: How shall we live?

Now I don't think that, in general, we see our lives like this. We take most of it 'for granted', as we say. We are very lucky if, in childhood and adolescence, we have questions we cannot answer. What usually happens is that parents and teachers are only too ready to give us *their* answers to *our* questions! Being young and easily impressed, we usually accept their answers and cease to search in ourselves. As we grow up we tend to bother about all these things less and less and so we end up living a life that is largely not our own, that has been imposed upon us – a sort of rubber-stamp life.

So the normal tendency of the young to question and discover life for themselves is often atrophied and discouraged – not always intentionally – by their elders, simply because we elders have a pattern, a way of thinking and acting, which has worked for us (we think) and it seems quite obvious to us it will work for them. But it is *our* pattern, not theirs. So the question: How shall we live? goes right back to the roots of our lives.

So what have we in life that is really our own?

III

'What have I in life that is really my own?' Don't be in a hurry to answer. If you leave the question lying about in your mind, as it were, and return to it from time to time, I think you will find it profitable. When we ponder, the discoveries are often unexpected.

But let us return to our theme, these good resolutions, which nearly always seem to come to nothing, and try to discover why. One part of us has looked at another, criticized it and decided to alter it. This is a principle of all spiritual growth. We are not as we should be: we should like to change. Very soon, if we look at ourselves like this, we shall see that our lives abound in such inner disagreements. The man we like today we can't stand tomorrow; the thing we longed for yesterday seems valueless today. And this continual fluctuation, these swings of our inner pendulum, are often accentuated by our digestion, or the weather, or the News. We are all familiar with this state of affairs. We know our moods change. Our good resolutions are really an attempt to control the fluctuations of our moods.

In all this we assume one thing, that there is a basic permanent part of us, a sort of label we call 'I', which is subject to these fluctuations. But is there this solid core? When I begin to examine my daily behaviour, all I find is that I continually stumble on *perceptions*. Perceptions of all kinds, continually chasing each other across the stage of my life, standing for a moment, claiming my attention and then disappearing, to turn up again an hour, a week, or perhaps a year later. When these perceptions stop, as in sleep, what exists? I am dead really, a perfect nonentity, until I wake. Then the flow of perceptions is resumed. So are we all nothing but our perceptions?

There is another aspect of all this which often passes unnoticed. Each actor on the stage claims, for a moment, my *whole* attention. There is nobody else there. Look and you will see how wholehearted you are: while you are gentle you are all gentleness; irritated you are all irritation, angry you are all anger. It amazes us ourselves when we see it afterwards. How could I have felt that? How could I have behaved like that? Our name is legion: we are many.

This way of looking at ourselves, sometimes called our

plurality or multiplicity, once we have seen it and begun to accept it as the true picture of what we call the 'self', is full of implications. One man commits a murder and all the other men in him spend a lifetime in gaol because of him. Slowly the responsibility of being a human being appears in quite a new light. The privilege carries a burden, the challenge implies a cross. Somehow we feel that if we could control this wild conglomeration of opposites in us, all of which call themselves 'I', we should be 'better' for it. But we can't. So bang go our good resolutions.

IV

If we take the word resolution apart and see it as the re-solving of a problem, it seems to add to its meaning. But there are overtones to the world. Resolution somehow means more than just resolving. Courage, determination and something worthwhile are all implied in the solid ring of the word resolution.

Indeed anyone who has observed his inner contradictions and resolved to grapple with them, certainly needs per-severance. But, at the same time, behind resolution, there is an urge, the mainspring of all struggle – and that is *wish*!

Wish lies at the heart of resolution. Not *want*, mind. Want is a light word, an indulgence of our desires; wish belongs to the deep places in us, to our *need*. The difference between what I want and what I need is an enticing red herring which could carry us way off target! So let us come back to wish.

We can't carry through anything important in life with-out really wishing to do so. If we do it with a light wish, or just a want, in nine cases out of ten, it will founder. So before we can begin this wonderful and enriching work of self-examination, we have really to wish to do so. Just casually to drift into it and out again will not only be useless to us but even increase our doubts and frustrations. For, make no mistake, he who decides to look at himself enters a labyrinth in which he will be many times dismayed before he reaches the heart of it.

However, there is still something else implied in this wonderful word resolution and that is *aim*. The very idea of solving something implies that all other ways have been rejected. We have found a direction towards solution, that is an aim. Aim and wish are body and soul of resolution.

So we begin to get into deep waters. And it's funny really when you come to think of it, that we should be so wary of looking at ourselves when, after all, what is so fascinating and remarkable in life as ourselves? I am the most unique and remarkable person I know! No doubt of it. Then why not look more closely and carefully at this paragon?

Because somewhere deep down in what we call our sub-conscious; but should, in my opinion, be called the super-conscious, we have a sneaking feeling that perhaps, only perhaps mind, we are not all we are cracked up to be. We've taken the odd look now and then and maybe, well maybe, better not tangle with it. There could be flaws.

Could it be that the face I show to the world is only a mask? Could it be that I know inside, I am not what I pretend to be? That I am a liar! But I want to believe – and I desperately want others to believe – that I am like this. My whole life is bound up with this need to be believed – and, underneath, it isn't true, and we know it.

V

To take all this any further I have to assume that you are open-minded, sufficiently disenchanted and dissatisfied with your life as it is to be ready to look for some other way of arranging it; that you are no longer prepared to be passive, trodden underfoot by events; but are resolved to grapple with the problem.

It would certainly be a good resolution to do so and I am only concerned to steer you towards it. We are being pushed to the edge of a precipice and the only way to escape disaster is to come to ourselves and see where we are going. Evidently all pacts and alliances, warnings and moralizings get us nowhere. We rapidly come to the conclusion that we can't believe anybody. Then what can we believe? We can believe and trust the ring of truth within ourselves – when we hear it and listen to it. The God inside us is not mocked.

You remember that question I put to you earlier: 'What have I that is really my own?' Let me rephrase it: 'How much of my life is just reaction to what is going on around me?' We are great reactors, and in the daily commerce of life it is certainly necessary to respond; but if we could look a little deeper into the way things are, maybe our response would be different. The way things are, the common nature of the whole, is not what we think it is. We have all equipped ourselves with 'personalized' spectacles through which to look at the world. So each of us sees it differently and all the views are distorted. This is not really how it is.

The pith, the core, the very essence of our good resolution is not to try to change ourselves or the world about us; but simply to take off our distorting glasses and see things as they are. We are very reluctant to do this and it is difficult to get them off. We are so used to them we feel lost without them. After a few seconds it is an enormous relief not to have to peer at things which look so different and come back to the cosy view we are used to. Yet, maybe, in those seconds I see something which astonishes me, because I recognize its truth and, maybe, if I persevere and look again and again I shall build up quite an album of snapshots of life, of my true self.

Now the effect of all this is, in one way, very sobering and disquieting because the reality, the truth about myself, well, it often isn't so hot. But, on the other hand, there comes with it a glorious and enormous sense of relief. I am not pretending any more. I am not hiding from myself. I am what I am. At last I have dared to look!

And do you think this is no great change? I tell you it is the beginning and end of the whole matter. I carry what I have seen back into life. I am changed by the truth I have seen and the more I see, the more I am.

VI

Where has all this thinking about good resolutions got us? There is certainly nothing new about the idea that a change of heart is the beginning of all change. But the trouble is that when we think about this, we say the 'world' must change, or 'they' must change. Never that *I* must change. I'm all right. And, anyway, what difference could it make for one person to change?

It is impossible for us to imagine how people of other ages lived. You have only to read a little history to realize that the way people thought and acted, the things they praised or condemned, the whole mode of thought of another age is incomprehensible to us. Our mode will be just as much of a mystery to generations to come. Already we begin to see something new. We are coming to the end of the worship of quantity, that there can always be more of everything. There can't. We see it, and are beginning to turn to quality. We are also coming to the end of our own arrogance, our idea that we can do everything, that Nature will obey us. It is only too clear that this a huge miscalculation. The more we meddle, the more everything gets snarled up. So, since human beings are everlastingly adaptable, we begin to look for some new way to make a richer life.

I am suggesting that one way is to begin to face yourself, to look and see how you really are, to question what you have always taken for granted, to *put yourself in doubt*. Of course, it is very difficult. People – and books – exist to help in the 'how' of all this. I am only concerned to stir the germ of the idea into life: How can a man know what he needs, if he doesn't know himself?

The world situation is beyond me; but can I find a new attitude towards it? What can replace the chaos, the madness? I don't know; but, maybe, if I look into myself, I shall see a chaos inside me which corresponds exactly to the chaos without. There is a famous saying: 'In order to be a good altruist you must first of all be an out-and-out egoist.' If you hope to set the world to rights, first set yourself to rights!

For what can stand against the tides of greed and power except the stronger tide of conscience rising in each one of us, to roll back the disastrous flood of anarchy and egoism that is rising all around us? The temporal is manifestly failing: we can see it every day. So we turn within, to the slow and painful rebirth of conscience; that there is a true morality with unchanging values; that the standard of life is more important than the standard of living. 'I came that ye might have life and might have it more abundantly.'

And it starts, this impulse towards abundance and re-creation, this impulse to understand and condone, to discover and pity; it starts right inside the heart and mind of each one of us. Look within. For such a good resolution, if it is strong enough and noble enough, can change the world. Nothing else can.

Chapter 13

Energy Crisis

I

What is energy? It is a very common word. We are always using it. 'He is very energetic', 'I have absolutely no energy', 'Don't waste your energy' and so on and so on. But what is energy? It seems to be a sort of power that all life stores up, manufactures in a way, and then spends or pours out, to get things done, to actualize processes, to live. Energy is the fuel of life.

One of the fascinating things about it is that, although we know very well how to spend it – and often waste it – we know far less about how to make it. The manufacture of energy is a long, secret, tedious process which we hardly see, although its expenditure is obvious. We are quite used to the idea that things run down and wear out; we seldom pause to consider that *living* things, if there were no building-up process, would quickly die. Death in fact occurs when an organism can no longer transform within itself the necessary energy to maintain life.

Now the efficiency of the running-down and winding-up process is beginning to be very important to us today. Society has just begun to see that, if it is not careful about how it spends energy, it will quickly run out of it. Many able and intelligent people are giving their attention to more efficient ways to use energy, in finding out thriftier ways to spend it and also to tap sources of it that will last longer.

One aspect of this efficiency is another idea with which we are all familiar: that the environment of living things is essential to their productive life. If we want to grow a good apple tree or a heavy wheat crop, we know we must pay careful attention to its position, its light, its watering, the nutrients in its soil, and so on. What it produces will depend very much on how we care for it.

99

We human beings get and spend energy just as much as any other living organisms do. How efficiently do we spend it? How much do we waste? It is something that is worth our attention, for we have greater possibilities than plants or animals. Opportunities are open to us to tap other sources of energy and to use them in the service of life. But do we recognize this? Does it interest us? And if we do, even in a vague sort of way, does it seem important to us?

The energy crisis looms large on the world horizon. How large does it loom on our personal horizon? I assure you that this question: How do I spend my energy? – which concerns us all, is every bit as important, more important, than its counterpart in outer life.

II

Where do we get our energy? Obviously from food. There are one or two interesting things about food. First, it all comes from outside us. It is something that belongs to a larger world which we can tap, as it were, to manufacture our own energy. It is the raw material of our personal processes. Second, this food is not all of the same kind. In the ordinary way we think of food as what we eat, what goes into our stomachs; but this is not the only food. We are all the time taking in two other kinds of food – the air we breathe and what we may call the vibrations that come from the life about us – our impressions of the world. Taken all together, the quality of the food we eat, the air we breathe and the sort of life we lead, constitute our total intake.

But the important thing is how we process these raw materials. We can think of ourselves as a chemical factory into which food comes and, on a sort of conveyor belt, passes through various changes inside us, being continually refined, building up in a series of marvellous transmutations, the energies by which we live. Taking this analogy a little further, we all know there are factories and factories. There are the efficient ones in which everything runs smoothly, where the management and the shop floor are in complete agreement and where an excellent end product shows a good profit on the investment; but there are others where such harmonious relationships do not exist, where the management is lazy and the machinery is rusty and poorly operated and where the whole organization barely pays its way.

We are all familiar with this state of affairs in the world around us and we can see very clearly the result of poor management and poor work on the general economy of society and the chances of a good life for the individual; but it does not occur to us, in general, to turn this analogy inside out and enquire into the efficiency, the harmonious development, of our personal factories, to ask ourselves if we are doing the best we can for ourselves and with ourselves, or even to consider what is the nature of the end product our factory turns out. We do not think of ourselves as factories at all – we are much too grand for that! – but when you come right down to it, that is what we are. We take in various kinds of food and we turn out – what?

The analogy breaks down, of course, as all analogies do, for *we* are the product of our own factory. What we *are* shows how our factory has worked. We make ourselves. Our aims and aspirations, our nature, our stature; in a word, our being – it is this we were born into this world to produce.

Now I suggest to you that, taking a look at the world around us and the manifestations of humanity today, there is a good deal of room for improvement in the way we use the energy we produce and the ends we put it to. We all have an energy crisis, no doubt about it. Where have we gone wrong?

III

When it comes to an energy crisis – or any other kind of crisis – we all do the same thing – blame the other chap! One is too lazy, another too greedy, a third too stupid, a fourth too cowardly, and so on and so on. But make no mistake about it – it cannot too often be stated – the world is what it is because we are what we are. If what we see about us is a terrible muddle and mess, it is because we, within ourselves, are in a terrible muddle and mess. We know it. Every day we repeat we cannot see an end to it all, we cannot find a way out and the sum total of all this personal inner chaos is the general chaos of society.

So what is to be done? We have to come back – as we must always come back – to ourselves. Everything begins there. How are we using all this energy we manufacture – or, if you like, how is it using us? To what end are we putting it? What is our aim? If our aim could be different, if this one thing could be different, all would be different. But it cannot. I am as I am. Things are what they are. The millennium will not appear overnight. But nevertheless there are trends, there are movements, possibilities. Nothing stands still. Our need is to find some way which will begin to reduce our inner contradictions, quiet our apprehensions, get us clear of the vortex which at every moment threatens to engulf us.

It is not easy to find this way. It is not easy to follow it when you have found it. It is not given to many to be able to pursue it, wholeheartedly, to the end. But we can all begin to look for it. We can all begin to ask ourselves: Does the way I live make sense? Where is it leading me? How am I spending my days – that is, how am I spending my energies?

I know these are difficult questions. Perhaps you do not really understand what I mean? You say: I spend my days as I must. I have my life to live, my responsibilities, my tasks. I cannot change all this. It is my situation. My destiny. What earthly use is it to me to tell me that my life might be different, or better. This is just preaching – and I'm tired of being preached at.

Quite right. I agree. It is my fault. I should have put it better. Of course you can't change your life. It is not even desirable that you should. But what you can change is your attitude towards it. By this I mean you can begin to change the way you look at it. You can keep tabs on it, analyse it, take it to pieces, so to speak, and see it for what it is.

And what good will that do me? you ask.

It will show you, if you persist, little by little, how you

spend your time and your energy. It will show you how little you know about your own life. It will show you, as somebody said to me the other day: 'I go on doing the same silly things in the same silly way.' It will show you that your own energy factory is just turning over, no more, making no profit, producing no growth for you as an individual.

It may be rather disturbing. It may put an end to some of your illusions about yourself. But you will have learned something. That often seems at first as if you had lost something.

IV

During about eight hours in the 24-hour cycle of our lives a large part of our energy factory closes down. Our communications with the outside world are cut, our normal activity rests. We sleep. But a lot is still going on. The body never sleeps. The heart pumps. The lungs breathe. The stomach digests. An exact temperature control is kept. A hundred and one miraculous interlocked processes continue, automatically, as we say; but in fact under the strict watch of the night manager and his staff, the most efficient and tireless division of our whole organization, our instinctive control centre.

During all this time the factory stores energy. Then we wake and begin to use it – and the trouble starts.

As I sit and ponder this, trying to make it clearer to myself so that I can pass it on to you, I really don't know where to begin. My thesis, my suggestion, is that the wrong use of energy, the waste of it, goes right down to the root of life. Our possibilities, our hopes, our longings, not even for a better life; but just for a normal one, are all brought to nothing by the way we waste our energies. All religions, and many philosophies, are geared to the proposition that, if we knew the right way to live, our troubles would be over. So what is the right way? It is a very loose question, for 'right' is open to a hundred interpretations. Let us shift it slightly and ask what is a *normal* way to live? After all there must be a norm. A lion lives the life of a lion. A mouse lives as mice live. A tree grows as trees grow. Why should man be an exception? He too must have his norm, his rightful place in the creation. But what is it?

It is an immensely complicated question. I can only answer it in part. It seems to me that a normal man would be one whose faculties and powers are fully developed, whose relationship with himself and the outside world are harmonious and whose aim is to serve life as a man should serve it. But clearly that is utopian. We don't get anywhere near that. Nevertheless it is a direction, an aim, towards which we have the right, the responsibility, to aspire. How can we begin?

For the moment I will take one part of this question – a simple, but very important part of it. When a man (or woman) is wholly absorbed in work, he is relatively safe. By 'safe' I mean he is using energy, not wasting it. Our organism is meant to work, to struggle, to develop its muscles, whether mental, physical or spiritual. Hard work never hurt anybody. We have all the energy we need for that.

The waste begins with idleness – 'the chief distress' as Henry VIII put it, 'of vices all!'

V

What is the relationship between idleness and the waste of energy? It would seem, at first sight, that when we are doing nothing, we must spend little or no energy. In fact the opposite is the case. When we are fully occupied in work, we must attend to it, and our attention acts like the governor on an engine which controls its speed. Take off the governor and the engine races.

Work limits the activity of our associations. We all have an astonishing computerized card index in our heads which exists to put together trains of associations – which we, in general, call 'thoughts' – in endless variety and infinite complexity. This computer cannot do anything else and never stops doing it. Arranging and re-arranging the material in our card index constitutes nearly the whole of what we call our 'thinking' life. When we are calm and have nothing much 'on our minds', the computer spins out webs of pleasant associations and we say that we 'day-dream'. Animals as well as men day-dream. It is a relatively harmless waste of time and energy.

Linked with our thinking card index is an emotional one, the place where our feelings are stored. Feelings are, in general, far more imperious and powerful than thoughts. We are, as we say, 'carried away' by our feelings. It is when these two begin to interact and feed on each other – as they almost always do – that the sluice gates are opened and our energy begins to pour out.

It is here that fantasy enters and with it, egoism. Thoughts and feelings, feeding on each other, build the whole world of illusion in which we live. It is this terrifying interaction that produces those states which we may call 'negative' emotions – since they are useless to us. Vanity, pride, anger, fear, depression, worry, these are the aspects of our self-justification that arise from our egoism, our self-love.

I have been trying to show you the mechanism of all this – how it happens. But it really doesn't matter. It is the end result that concerns us, the state in which we spend so much of our lives, a totally useless and self-destructive state, which leads to violence, murder and war on the one hand, and to frustration, neurosis, illness and madness on the other. And all this arises from the fantastic misdirected use of energy, which our patient bodies build for us nightly – until they break down from exhaustion.

So again comes the old cry – what can we do about it?

This is a problem about which you can do something that is simple, practical and very much to the point. You can refuse yourself the luxury of manifesting your negative emotions. If you are angry, don't show it. If you feel critical, or bitter, or hurt, or depressed, don't show it. Don't feed it. Bottle it up inside you and don't let go even if you are ready to burst. This will show you many things – how much energy you are wasting on them, how full your life is of these negative states and last, but best of all, how ephemeral they are, once you stand up to them.

For the tiger of anger, the turkey of vanity, the elephant

of depression, the whole menagerie that obsesses you, will turn out, ten minutes later, to be no more than dead flies. Try it, and you will see.

VI

I have been trying to put before you a very simple, basic proposition: We live by taking in food and then we waste the best part of the energy it gives us. But do we ever think of life like this? We enjoy our 'ordinary' food, we may even realize it is better to breathe fresh air than stale (though we don't call it the food it is) and today we may even have begun to glimpse that the environment, the impressions that come to us from life are important – when we can take them in. But, in general, we pay little attention to how our factory runs. We misuse it and so it doesn't produce anything like what it could.

Once we look at our days, we cannot fail to see how they are spent: the trouble is we don't want to look. It is our dreams that interest us. The reality is lost beneath them. Today, for instance, where do my thoughts run? Criticisms on the shortcomings of my wife, on the difficulties with my colleagues, the stupidity of my boss, on the way I got the better of X yesterday and how much Y admires me for it. Or, maybe, the boredom of my job, the depression of the weather or the fact that nobody, but nobody, seems to see how much more able and remarkable I am than those I work with. The details vary, but this is what it adds up to. We are all obsessed with ourselves and usually frustrated by our situation and our consolation is to escape from it altogether into a book, or the telly, or the football pools, or drink – anything to take us away from life as it is. So, as a result, the hospitals and prisons are overcrowded, half the world is at the other half's throat, while anarchy and the hydrogen bomb wait in the wings.

Nobody can fail to see this is the way it is going, if they dare to look. It is all pretty depressing and there seems no way out. But there must be a way out. Life does not stop. Even if some maniacs start pressing buttons and the world is blown up, something will survive and life will start again. The Everlasting Mercy can accept a few fireworks.

But why should it come to this? Can we not begin to see that all our energies are being misdirected, put to no constructive use and are mortally wounding us and our fellow men – and indeed the whole world? So I suggest to you it is time to take stock of our situation, to see if we cannot begin to stem this mad Niagara of wasted energy.

But how, how, how?

It is very difficult; but I try. I try to turn in another direction. I try to hold on to myself, not to get sucked into the vortex. I try, desperately, to be quiet, to be still, to honour the God within me. I begin to value my own inner peace and refuse to be at the mercy of this world outside which constantly tries to seduce me.

It is hard. I continually fail. I am always tripping and falling. But that does not matter, so long as I get up.

I feel energy building up within me. I am full of life. And now? What shall I do with this energy now I have saved it?

Ah, that is another matter. But the great thing is to begin to try to save this energy. To begin! Now!!

Chapter 14

The Law of Three

I

Wherever we are and whoever we are, old or young, rich or poor, man or woman, we all face this day which is now beginning in an identical situation. And this situation is made up of three parts, three ingredients, three components: how do I face myself, how do I face my colleagues, how do I face my life?

How *do* I face myself? It's an odd sort of question and not one I am in the habit of asking. I am what I am and I take myself 'for granted', as we say. Still, when I do happen to look, I would admit there are fluctuations. Some mornings I am irritable and depressed, some I am buoyant and optimistic. Sometimes I dread the day ahead, sometimes I look forward to it. It all depends on how I *am* this morning, and I know, from experience, that it is sometimes possible to better my state, to 'pull myself together' – as if 'I' was not myself and I could divide, see and change myself, stand in a different relation towards myself. And I know, also from experience, that if I can do this, it certainly shows result in the day ahead.

It will certainly affect the second component: my relations with colleagues or neighbours. Some of us like people, get on with them and accept their shortcomings or idiosyncrasies. '*Vive la différence!*' as the French say. Others are on the defensive, intolerant, frightened, wanting everybody to behave as they do. Some of us are leaders and have the faculty of inspiring those about us, some are 'hail fellow well met' with all and sundry, some are loners and just do not like people at all, or know not how to make contact with them. There are infinite gradations. But we could all agree, I think, that the better my own state, the better my relation with others is likely to be. The two things are interdependent.

And then there is the job, the project, on which I and those working with me are engaged. It is bigger than we are, more remote; but it holds us together. It compels our interest, maybe our loyalty and nobody needs to be told it will succeed or fail according to what we put, or don't put, into it.

So there are these three components and they make up the bulk of our lives. They are not separate, fixed, static. They continually interpenetrate one another and change position. Sometimes one man can inspire others to put a job through; sometimes, as in social changes, people themselves take the lead and sweep the leader up to effect the reform; sometimes the aim, the ideal, is so compelling that it pulls the world after it. At every level, on every scale, from the family to the world situation there is this continual interplay of three forces, I, my neighbour and my aim. It is like some everlasting dance. The dance of life.

II

Most of us hold pretty decided views about things and the idea that in every situation there are always three ingredients, is not one, I think, that is generally held. The normal point of view – normal because most people hold it – is that there are two. Things, we say, are right or wrong, true or false, good or bad, black or white, and this attitude that there are always two opposites, is the way we see the world around us. It has been called the dualistic world and every religion has consistently told us that it is not true, that this is the world of illusion. There are always three forces, three ingredients they say; but such is the power of our ingrained habits of thought that we don't see it this way. We are third-force blind.

Let us take an obvious instance. I have written these words and you are reading them; but what I have written, what holds us together, is neither me nor you. The idea, the thought, is the bond which unites us. But the fact escapes us. We don't see life that way. We know perfectly well that we live in a three-dimensional world; but we think dualistically, as if we were flat-earth men. So truth, reality, always eludes us. It could be the reason for the mess we are in. Dualism is not enough.

If this idea, which is a basic reality of the Universe, happens to excite you, you can find a thousand examples of it around you every day. How could there be any day or night if the Earth did not spin? How many chemical combinations cannot take place without the presence of a catalyst? Light occurs when the positive and negative electrical forces pass through the lamp. Life consists of chains of 'events' and in each one there are always three forces.

To illustrate the manner in which these forces change places in what I have called the 'dance of life', let us isolate a very popular event – a general election. In every election there are three main components – the policies, the candidates and the voters. In the run up to the election, the policies of the rival parties are all important – active. We, the voters, listen to them and consider them – we are passive. The exponents, the candidates, mediate between policy and voters, explaining, exhorting and so on. They are the reconciling force.

But come polling day, the roles change. We passive voters become active. We decide. The candidates can now do nothing. They are passive, awaiting our verdict. This verdict we give on the strength of the policies which now hang in the balance, the neutralizing or equalizing force.

After it is all over, the candidates go to Parliament and become (we hope) active in implementing the policies, which are passive, and we voters take up a mediating role, commenting and criticizing the parties as they swing this way and that, carrying out, or not carrying out, their promises.

Of course, this is an over-simplification. You cannot isolate one event from all the others that impinge on it. It is a labyrinth in which we easily get lost. But always because we project on to reality a dualistic habit of thought, which can never make sense.

There is nothing new in this triadic view of things. The triangle, the symbol of the three forces, is very ancient.

You find it in the Star of David, you find it in the ruins of Zimbabwe, in the Pyramids of Egypt. You find it in the three 'gunas', or forces, of the Hindus. You find it here in the West in what we call the Holy Trinity.

III

Some of you may perhaps be shocked at my associating the Holy Trinity with the mundane events of everyday life. I come myself of a religious stock. My beloved father and grandfather were both Ministers of the Church. So I was accustomed in childhood to regular churchgoing and the invocation of the Holy Trinity, especially at the Benediction, never failed to move me. There was a wonderful ring to the words. As if I knew, without knowing, that there was something there. Later, in a more literal and sceptical period, I grew to regard the words as a sort of mystical incantation. It made no sense to me at all – particularly the Holy Ghost. Ghosts, to me, were rather eerie creatures, insubstantial, and not at all holy. What were they doing at the culmination of Divine Service?

It was not until middle age that I happened to discover a teaching which postulated, among other marvellous things, the existence of a Law of Three as one of the two Primordial Sacred Laws of the Universe, created by God, the Prime Source of Everything Existing. The Law of Three! No sooner had I heard about it than the idea lodged in my mind like a dagger. It shot through the darkness of my understanding like a meteor. I found myself saying 'Yes! Yes!', seized by the truth of it and putting together from a thousand associations, instances in the world around me of how this coming together of three forces constituted every event. This was the Holy Trinity in action.

Up till then for me, as for most people, three had been no more than a lucky number. That was all there was left, the minute tip of an iceberg that, in reality, motivated everything from the whirling vortex of the Pleiades to the dance of the atoms in the molecule. Everything, but everything, obeyed this Sacred Law.

So religion – which, to many, is almost a dirty word today – came shouting down from the altar into life! My life, your life, into the life of science and industry, into the life of art and politics, into every corner of the market-place of life. The Trinity was no longer a mystical euphoria, a sort of mumbo-jumbo for Sundays. It was a plain, verifiable fact. The Word was made Law and dwelt among us.

Of course, at first, it was no more than an intellectual exercise to try to see it. But those who patiently instructed me, begged me to search for the working of this Sacred Law within myself. For, to the extent that I could understand it, I should understand reality. My own reality and therefore, since I too am a Universe in miniature, the reality of the world.

We must strive to understand. The Triad is omnipresent. It is not enough for the Sacred to touch our hearts. Today we need it to excite our minds, bite us, until we long to be.

Meanwhile here is another invocation of the Trinity from the works of my teacher.

> Holy Affirming!
> Holy Denying!
> Holy Reconciling!
> Transubstantiate in me
> For my Being.

Chapter 15

Operation Hope

I

I often think that not the least remarkable thing about Churchill's life was the manner in which, towards the end of it, he planned the final ceremonies by which his death should be commemorated. To be so objective and yet so practical as to allow the living mind to contemplate the rituals following its own end is a mark of greatness such as it is not given to many of us to reach. He called this plan, I believe, 'Operation Hope Not', and the terrible finality of the phrase led me to the realization of the enormous part Hope plays in all our lives.

We do not realize, I think, the extent to which hope colours all we do and say. We hope it will be fine tomorrow, or that the deal on which we are engaged will move towards a successful conclusion; we hope that our health will be better or that our relations with the family or the neighbours will improve; we hope that our horse will win or that we shan't catch a cold. We hope, in short, for a happy outcome to our lives and, in a very strange way, however often our hopes are dashed, we at once adjust them or change their focus and so manage to maintain a buoyancy, a resilience, without which, it seems, we should find it almost impossible to go on living. Nobody who contemplates it for a moment can fail to be impressed at the way in which, faced by disaster after disaster, people find this extraordinary capacity to hope.

But there is something about hope which we all take for granted and that is the way it is always attached to our desires. We always hope *in* something. Hope is a pair of rose-coloured spectacles through which we view our future. It is a sort of bias we give to our possibilities. It is the sugar icing we put on our intentions, our wishes, our plans. It does not seem to exist by itself. You cannot hope in a vacuum.

Yet, at the same time, hope is a very subjective thing. It is different for each of us. It is a sort of reaching out towards something beyond us, which does not yet exist, but still might exist. There is an element of prayer in it.

So the question arises: What do I hope for myself? What do I want for myself? Are there legitimate hopes – hopes beyond my own egoism? Is there an 'Operation Hope' beyond Churchill's 'Operation Hope Not'?

II

Hope is something always in the future: you cannot hope in yesterday.

It is attached to our 'doing', to our commerce with life; that is, it is attached to our *personality*. But is our personality all of us? Or is there another part, something more subtle, more deeply hidden in us than what appears as personality, something which itself colours personality and influences it?

I am going to suggest to you that there is. In fact that there is an idea here, so basic, so fundamental, that beginning to try to understand it is really a master key to one of the great mysteries in human behaviour. This idea does not exist, as far as I know, in any other teaching other than the one I have been studying for the last thirty years, and it is simply this: We all consist of two parts: our essence and our personality. What do I mean by this? What is our essence? What is our personality?

We are all familiar with the word essence. It conveys to us the idea of a concentrate. We talk about the essence of an idea or of a situation. 'These are my essential needs'. 'The essence of the whole question boils down to this' - and so on and so on. What is essential is the heart, the core of the matter. If then I say that I have an essence, that you have an essence, it is meant to convey the idea that hidden at the bottom of our lives is something which makes each one of us different from every other and this something is not acquired by us through contact with life; but is born with us into life. It is our individual spark of life itself, our divine part, if you like, our embryonic soul.

We are now, all of us, more or less familiar with the ideas of genetic inheritance, with the extraordinary discovery of the double helix, which shows – among other things – how every single one of us has a distinct and separate basic genetic structure – of amazing complexity – a sort of key in which lies the shape of all the possibilities that are open to us in this life. This is the essential me, the essential you. Our essence.

But how does this essence relate to personality? And how does it all relate to hope? We seem to have changed direction from the subject we started to explore. Well, perhaps not so far as you think.

III

This individual blueprint we all carry from the moment of conception, the template, so to speak, on which we can build our lives, the projected shape of things to come, is alive, so it begins to grow; but the *way* it grows, the extent to which it grows, depends on the circumstances of the life around it and it is the life around it which determines the personality.

Personality is something absolutely different from essence. It does not come from the inside, the source of life; but is impressed on to our lives by the influence around us. We start, if you like, as a clean sheet of paper on which those around us begin to write. Mothers write, fathers write, brothers, sisters, friends, relations, all write. And all this writing, these outside impressions, are recorded in our thoughts, feelings, and habits, in a very complex way. These are the influences which from the moment of birth – and before – begin to form our personality. They are not ours; but we record them and we are so made that we remember them, store them, rearrange them and subsequently bring them out *as if they were our own*.

If we happen to be surrounded by loving parents and friends, if our lives are interesting and comfortable, we shall record those kinds of impression. If we are subject to unhappy

circumstances, to angry, violent or discontented people,
we shall inevitably be influenced by that sort of life. Of
course circumstances alter cases. There may be one very
strong influence in childhood which swamps all the others.
There may be something in our genetic inheritance so
powerful it eclipses everything else; but, in general, the
personality we emerge with at maturity, is compounded of
an extremely complex set of impressions we have recorded
in our personal private computers.

So we face life with an immensely complicated set of
recordings, of which we cannot recall one hundredth
part. Beneath lies a very subtle, almost unknown blueprint of our tendencies, the sort of person we really are, or
could be.

Often these two parts are in conflict. Small wonder if we
cannot make head nor tail of our situation.

IV

Only very rarely do essence and personality remain in
balance. That is, only very rarely do our inner and outer
lives develop harmoniously. What usually happens is that
the pull of outside life is so strong that it smothers our inside
life and takes the centre of the stage. Our personality
eclipses our essence.

Yet essence is our birthright, born into life with us, the
form of our life itself, our genetic heredity. Our personality
on the other hand, is a hotchpotch of carefully recorded
ideas, feelings and habits, not our own; but because we
never pause to think about all this, taken for our own,
seemingly original, and so constantly in the foreground
in our daily living that we end up by trusting them absolutely,
and thinking indeed that our personality is all we have.

Think of it if you like, as our body being the essence and
the clothes we wear our personality. The body grows, or
can grow; but the clothes do not and cannot. They are just
things we put on to face life with. And we can change them.
In fact we are always changing them. Have you not one
suit you wear when you talk with your wife or husband?

Have you not quite another when you talk to your boss, another for your colleagues, another for your lover, another for the man who cuts in ahead of you on the road? If you look, you cannot fail to see how you change your attitude, your voice, your vocabulary, with lightning rapidity to meet each change of circumstance – you even change your memories to suit each part!

Now it does not at all follow that our over-developed personalities have anything in common with our essence. Indeed the opposite may be the case. How often do we read of people whose lives have finally become so foreign and hateful to their natures, that they ultimately rebel, even have breakdowns, and turn from what they have been doing to something totally different. Their smothered essence has finally refused to allow the dressed-up dummy of personality to rule their lives, to ruin what they really are.

Now do you begin to see how Hope comes into all this? For our hopes are attached to our personalities, to the part of us that is not really us. Daily life has swamped, squashed, the only part of us that is really our own, the part of us that might genuinely hope. It is a sort of death in life. So what is to be done in such a desperate situation?

V

If we had been rightly brought up, properly educated, these two parts of ourselves, our essence and our personality, would have been harmonized, our outer and inner lives brought into relation with each other. Then our priorities would be saner, our values clearer, and there would be genuine objective hope for all of us.

Sometimes when people begin to see this basic division in themselves, they want to condemn personality altogether, because it is a fraud, a fake, and they jump to the conclusion that if they could live solely in essence, they would be living in truth and the problem would be solved. But we cannot do this. We are two-natured. We cannot throw away our personalities any more than we can go about daily life in the nude. We need our clothes to be able to carry on with outer life; we need our essence to develop our inner life. This conflict is our birthright. It is also our cross. Life on Earth is – and is meant to be – struggle. Struggle between what I do and what I am.

But how are we to all this today? We have forgotten everything but our clothes. We live for appearances. Yet, at the same time, we are finding there is something wrong with it. It is evidently promoting all kinds of dissatisfactions and conflicts inside ourselves – and therefore in society. There could not possibly be the violence, the greed, the egoism of life around us today if we realized what was wrong. We are all flailing about, shouting 'This is the solution', 'That is what we ought to do', crying, as in the Gospels, Lo here and Lo there. But the Kingdom of Heaven is within us.

And this Kingdom of Heaven is the domain of the essence, of the unalterable Divine Shape with which we were born and which we ignore, not so much deliberately, but simply because we have forgotten it exists, because nobody has ever told us about it. Told us about it, not in some pious exhortation from the pulpit, but as a basic, incontrovertible, scientific fact. The double helix of our essence is far nearer the truth than all the slogans dreamed up by our personalities. Communism, fascism, democratic socialism, none of these can ever set the world to rights while the individual essence in each of us is imprisoned.

So how can we hope and in what can we hope? There is no more important question before us all.

VI

Yet we must be on guard, careful how we hope and for what we hope. There is a disastrous snare before us here. The things that I ought to do today often seem difficult. It would be much easier, much better, I feel, if I put them off till tomorrow. So there is an element of procrastination in hope. It is a sort of illness we all have, a general epidemic, and has been called 'the disease of tomorrow'. The disease of putting off from day to day the effort that should be made, the decision that should be taken, the fundamental essential step without which there can be no hope.

And what is this fundamental step? It is the resolve to come back to myself. Now. Even while I am speaking. To look into myself and ask: How am I? Now. What do I need? Now. Where am I going? Now. And, as we struggle to do this, we begin to see that all our lives – lived as they are in our personalities – we have given respect to that which is not respectable and our inner life, which is worthy of respect, we have left out on the doorstep, like an orphan. We have to come back to this poor neglected creature and consider its needs, which are ours, to consider its rights, which we have forgotten, to consider its place, which is the eternal fire at the heart of life.

For the essential life in me, the essential life in you, the double helix of every life, is only a *possibility*. It does not at all follow that such possibilities will be realized. In fact, by ignoring and squashing – and even killing – this part of us, that is, by living only in our personalities, we deprive ourselves of the only part of us that is worthy of faith and love and hope.

Daily life must be lived – yes. Daily struggle must be made – yes. But unless we set aside a time, every morning and every evening, when we try to shut out the world and its boisterous cacophony, and patiently, carefully, persistently, search for and nourish this orphan, there can be no hope for us – such as we are.

So now! Try! Shut out your noisy world. Be content only to follow your breathing or the quiet relaxation of your limbs. Sit in the heart of yourself, fighting for stillness, and, if you persist, day by day, you may certainly hope to reach that point of peace which is the eye of the hurricane. What more need you hope for in this life?

Chapter 16

Is There an Afterlife?

I

It is what is called, in current terms, the 64,000 dollar question. But, unlike the competition, where a verifiable answer is sometimes forthcoming, this question can never be answered. That is the first thing to get clear. For, in a curious way, although we know it, we continue to hope against hope that someone will come up with an answer.

Why do we want to know so much? Why has the question obsessed mankind since the dawn of time? Partly, I think, it is our egoism. Every man's life is so important to him. He has worked so hard, suffered so much, struggled so bravely, it seems unfair, irrational, such a waste, that all his accumulated knowledge, experience, wisdom, should be just blotted out. He simply cannot face extinction. If it all ends in oblivion, why struggle at all?

Yet he must. Something impels him. He is so made that he must strive, exercise his powers, help himself and his fellow men. This alone gives meaning, inspiration, to his life. Then is it not justice that, at the end of it, he should be rewarded, given the chance of some further opportunity? He cannot believe that *his* effort, *his* contribution, is no longer wanted. In the Christian tradition where we postulate a loving Father who cares for us personally, it is really inadmissable for *me* to be cast aside – patient, long-suffering, hard-working me. That really would be a dirty trick. It cannot be true.

But, leaving all the egoism aside, it does seem that people, some people, at any rate, do *grow* in the course of their lives. We may have seen examples of it among friends or acquaintances, individuals who, as a result of experiences they have passed through – usually tragic – have somehow developed in a way that is difficult to define, but can quite clearly be *felt* by those around them. It is not just what they have

massed as life experience, it is something else, an attitude
owards things, a way they are able to BE before life.

In a curious way, when we are with such people, we *feel*
a certain quietness, an acceptance. Not resigned, for that
would mean they didn't care. It is as if their suffering had
not turned – as it so often does – to self-pity; but had somehow been transmuted to what we sometimes call spiritual
merit. They stand calmly before life with open hands and
take what comes. It is as if there were two people there.
The ordinary everyday person and this inner person who
is not touched.

Could it be this separate, inner person who has the chance
to continue to live when the ordinary person is dust?

II

Sometimes a problem can best be solved by examining
ourselves, sometimes it helps to look at the world around us.
Even a glance at this shows us many things; but one thing
we cannot ignore – the amazing prodigality of Nature. It
seems as if all life were based on the principle of massive
over-production, of gargantuan waste.

I live on an island where there are several million olive
trees. Their fruit runs into billions upon billions of olives.
Even though some are harvested, I have never yet seen a
single seedling growing under all those trees, yet the possibilities are there. What happens to all the olives that do not
germinate? They fall and rot and their dissolution provides
food by which the trees continue to live.

It is somewhat the same within us. A continuous process
of death and rebirth takes place inside us. Our body cells
live a very short time, perhaps a few seconds, nothing
compared with our human life span. They are continually
carried away by the blood. Some are burned and evaporate
out of the system. Some, it seems, in a mysterious way,
participate in the birth of new tissue. But there are also
'immortal' cells, such as brain cells, that last as long as our
life lasts, cells that are immortal within the human cosm

There is a very old saying 'As above, so below'. Th

that operate on one scale operate on all others. Is it too
fanciful to suppose that the cells in my body also have
problem about their afterlife? Immortality for them woul
be to become a cell of my head brain and participate in th
direction of the Universe that is me. Whether it is so or no
it is clear that for all the myriads that die, few can fin
place there.

You remember the parable of the sower and the seed. O
all that was sown, very little came to fruition, to harvest, onl
the possibilities were there. This is a very curious parable
Is our immortality a matter of luck, of where we happen t
fall in life? Or is there something beyond luck, in the ver
throwing, that decides how the seed shall fall?

How can we know the answer to such questions? W
can only ponder them and wonder. Is it possible that m
chances of another life depend on the way I have lived thi
one? Many would agree that this had something to do wit
it. But do we care about an afterlife enough to bother
Maybe it is all a hoax.

III

In spite of the wars and persecutions that have bloodie
its history from the Crusades to the Inquisition, Christianit
remains a teaching of love. Because of this it differs radicall
from other religions in many respects. It produces a ver
personal relationship between man and his Maker. Go
cares for the Christian personally, guides him personally
intercedes and pardons him personally and because of a
this love, it becomes very easy to believe that, after death
he is guaranteed a personal afterlife.

So, although almost every parable in the Gospels makes i
perfectly clear that any future life depends on the way w
behave in this one, there is a general tendency to gloss thi
over and – because of our egoism again – to imagine tha
we haven't done so badly and that we shall probably ge
by.

What gets by? Because death is not a subject on which w
like to dwell and because there is no valid answer to th

riddle, the whole area remains rather foggy, a field for all manner of imagination and conjecture. We are doing it now.

When a car runs out of petrol, it stops. All the intricate mechanism ceases to function. It dies. But the petrol is not the car and indeed has nothing in common with it. It is much finer matter than steel or plastic. Yet without it the car is so much scrap.

In much the same ways when life withdraws from any living creature, it ceases to perform the functions for which it was created. All life is subject to this law. Everything that is born into time obeys it. The swallow and the elephant, the whale and the orchid, all things whatsoever are continually dying and being reborn. A 'something' we call life is continually surging into the whole creation – and just as continually withdrawing from it again. It seems more like some invisible electric current than anything else which, passing into and out of every created form, lights it for a moment with what we call 'life' and passes on.

Looked at like this our personal destiny seems irrelevant, incidental. We see around us the miraculous interlocking ecology of organic life. Everything is keyed into everything else, depends on everything else, feeds on everything else. Out of an infinite diversity it achieves unity. It is all one. And no sentient person can behold it without knowing it is inspired by the Creator in an act of love.

Or perhaps an act of reason inspired by love. For surely it is impossible to look on the beauty of it all without being in awe at the Divine Intelligence that created it. Reason is here as well as love. But it had not only to be created, it has also to be maintained. Does the Creator do all this Himself, or does He need helpers. May not the aspiration of man be to be worthy to offer such help, to become, say, an archangel?

IV

Here I am, an insignificant little man, facing this Goliath question: 'Is there an afterlife?' I cannot know; but I must use my powers, feeble as they are. As I ponder, it seems fairly clear that the body cannot continue, for i decays and disappears. But the 'something' we call life, i not the body. Does that persist? Has it, like some electri current, always been there, and will it always continue t be there, an eternally circulating force which, as we say 'breathes into man the breath of life'.

It seems, in some ways, a plausible hypothesis; but it i dreadfully impersonal. If the life-force is just some curren driven by a Divine Dynamo, there is no personal place fo you and me in it. Our hopes for the future, in some form or other, go out of the window. Yet somehow, in some deep unthinking 'knowing', a belief persists that it is not quite like that. The individual 'soul', as we think of it, persists and continues to live in a way we cannot apprehend until, perhaps, it returns again, reclothed in another body.

Worn out garments
Are shed by the body.
Worn out bodies are shed
By the dweller within the body.
New bodies are donned by the dweller, like garments.

This is how the Hindus put it. There is, they say, this dweller within the body, not an undifferentiated spark – but an immortal part which returns again and again to the struggle of life.

This idea of return, of reincarnation as it is called, may be no more than a doom of eternal repetition. I come back to live exactly the same sort of life, making the same mistakes, being caught in exactly the same way by my previous limitations. BUT, there is always the *possibility* of avoiding some of those mistakes. In other words there is always the possibility of *growth*.

Just as the sapling grows to be a tree or the child grows to be a man, so this immortal part can grow and the aim o growth is finally to free oneself from this cycle of repetition, to graduate, as it were, to quite another kind of life. 'To no more returning', as the Buddha put it, 'when this life is over'.

Do you ever get tired of yourself? Do you never see yourself, like some mechanical toy, doing the same stupid things in the same stupid way over and over again? I know I do. The idea of being condemned to continue for ever, returning again and again, to the same failings, the same limitations, that seems more like Hell than Heaven. This is how it is doomed to be, say the Hindus, without struggle.

Is this way of thinking a valid belief? I don't know – but I know one thing quite clearly. If the future holds no prospect of *growth*, I want no part in it.

V

It is the Resurrection that is responsible for the Christian idea of a personal life in the body, beyond the grave. The entire Passion may be seen as a deep allegory; but, if we take it literally, at its 'face value' – as many do – I have always wondered if it follows that because such a possibility was open to Jesus, it is open to the rest of us, such as we are.

Jesus was certainly no ordinary being. He had divine powers, powers we call miraculous because they transcend anything we as humans can encompass. If He wished to show us something by his Resurrection, He was able to do so. But we have no such powers. We cannot even withstand life, how can we then expect to withstand the terror of death, and overcome it?

Although there are many references in the Gospels to eternal life, I have never been able to find any suggestion, or promise, that such a life was connected with the body. There seems to have been something very naïve about the way the teaching was laid down in the early days. Surely it is a big jump, an extraordinary assumption, that because Jesus displayed such miraculous powers, we could all do the same, that it was the good man's destiny?

I suppose because I have a very 'low grade', practical mind, I find I cannot accept this, as it stands. My logic interferes. Something I feel, must be missing. Some key to what all this means. I cannot take it literally. For, I say to myself, if it is true, there must be a 'somewhere' in which all these myriads and myriads of good men continue to exist. What do they do? What is the purpose of their continued life? Do I, an old man, want to continue to live for ever, as an old man? Certainly not.

We all love life. Enough, at any rate, to wish for it to continue. The Church has played on this fear of dying by assuring us that, if we live an 'upright' life, we stand a good chance of an even better life – in the body – in the hereafter. I cannot find chapter and verse for this. I cannot believe that Jesus, who taught so simply and profoundly ever imagined that his Passion could give rise to such a fairy-tale.

The Gospels are full of directions and exhortations to all men and women as to how to live their lives in a becoming way, how to struggle to realize their longings. In a word, how to *grow* to something beyond their present powers of understanding. Growth is a law of life.

If a man works honestly and persistently at his life's tasks, it seems that, parallel with his outer effort, an inner growth begins. That 'something' which is essentially his, is nourished by this effort. This core, his essence, which was born with him, may at the end of life be more than it was at the beginning. The possibility of such an immortality is there.

VI

To conclude our attempt to explore this, the most baffling of all questions, let us try to pull our speculations together into some sort of order.

We recognize there is a 'something' born with every creature. It appears at birth: it disappears at death. I inspires our life; but is separate from it. This indwelling force, which we call 'life', is not just an undifferentiated current flowing in and out. Each life has a drop of it, so to speak, carrying within itself all our possibilities of growth.

It is this possibility of growth which sets us apart from the rest of the earthly creation. Our imperfection is our urge. Out of our *doubts* grows this inner division between what could be and what is. So, today, we see ourselves swaying between the lowest and basest of human manifestations and the highest. The pendulum swings. The worse things are, the better they must become. So when all's wrong, all's right.

The Great Originator, the Prime Source, set the whole Universe in motion. But He participated only at the beginning. Once created, it developed according to the Laws He had devised for its continuance. In a way, it passed beyond His control – as you may bear a child and cannot, to a large extent, determine how it will grow up. God created the world and its proliferation through galaxies and solar systems, through suns, planets and moons, down to the organic life, men, molecules and atoms, which followed.

The further it proceeded from Him, the more complex it became and so, because we are a long, long way away from Him, our life is beset with complications. But all this Divine Organization has to be guided, guarded, maintained, like any other organization. It is not infallible. It is alive, growing, and things that are growing can go wrong.

So here enters a new concept of immortality. The teacher needs the pupils as much as the pupils need the teacher. It is two-way traffic. We could not feel the need of God, if He had no need of us. He created us with the possibility of giving him help in a growing world. He needs us. Therefore He calls us. Whether we answer or not is our responsibility.

So we must face our life – and death – not fearfully, begging for some personal immortality – a pair of wings and a place in the choir – but positively, practically, aiming, hoping, believing that, at the end of it, we may be worthy to serve Him in some greater work we can never know nor discern. If a man lives his life for himself alone, it will certainly wither; if he lives it in the service of God, it must certainly grow.

Chapter 17

Safari

I NEED

I thought that in this section we might set out together on an exploration, an enquiry, a sort of safari into the inner life. Although the country is wild, there are camp grounds we can name as we come to them; but our starting point, our base camp, is quite a big busy centre. It is called Need.

I assume you would not be reading this kind of book unless you hoped to get something from it; and if you want something, it follows you cannot be entirely satisfied with life as it is and yourself as you are. You want something even if you don't quite know what it is. You are in Need. Now this is a very healthy state. It is the Divine Discontent, immortalized in that verse from the Omar Khayyam:

> *Ah, love! could thou and I with Fate conspire*
> *To grasp this sorry scheme of things entire*
> *Would we not shatter it to bits, and then*
> *Remould it nearer to the heart's desire!*

That about sums it up, the longing we all feel at one time or other, for something new and better which would lead us to a state of perfection. But, at some point, we have to commit ourselves, leave our base camp, Need, and set out. It is then the adventure starts, for then we ask ourselves what is the nature of this 'sorry scheme of things entire'? Well, it's a pretty big question. And, if we press on to try to discover the nature of our 'heart's desire' – what do I want – now! – can we answer . . . ? The impulse, the wish, however genuine, remains a dream, cloud-cuckoo-land, and so we sit at base, sighing at the impossibility of it all, resigned to getting on as best we can with this imperfect life as it is.

But that is a counsel of despair, to lie down under life! Life is terrible, wonderful! How can we grapple with it ignorant of its mystery? And you, I, aren't we mysteries to

128

ourselves? The one is a reflection of the other and the relationship between the two, that is between us and life, is the nub of the whole matter. Need is the starting point, the impulse; but to set out, to enquire, explore, needs effort. To want is cheap; to wish costs money. How can we remould life, if we don't understand it? Look what a mess the so-called 'experts' are making of it! And as for self-knowledge! We know nothing about ourselves. We don't even know how to look!

If you don't feel the challenge in all this, if you are perfectly satisfied with life as it is and yourself as you are, then obviously this safari is not for you; but if dissatisfaction and frustration put you on your mettle, rouse you into an active life, to try to discover if there is not some way to *be* towards all this, to face the hazards, the difficulties, the thrills of the journey – then we can set out. The first leg is quite a short one, a sort of suburb of Need. It is called Search – and there are some very lively people camping there!

II SEARCH

There are a lot of interesting people in Search, people who are all actively looking for something. It is a straggling sort of place; but there is an air of excitement about it. There are groups of people looking for new hypothesis, new facts, new techniques. There are others looking for personal things, vocations, careers, or just money. Our lot, those who are searching for something they can hardly define, a key to the understanding of life, are thought by the rest to be barmy. Chiefly because we are searching for something we think we have lost, whereas they are after something new.

Are we right? Have we lost something? Had we at one time some connection, some contact with a truth, a certainty, which, with the passing of years, has got buried under the rubbish dump of daily life? Wordsworth thought we had. 'Trailing clouds of glory do we come,' he said, 'From God who is our home.' If these 'clouds of glory' are only hidden, are they what we are looking for? Looking when we have time, mind. Don't let's kid ourselves. We are so busy with this and that, we have only time to give it all a glance now and then. We don't spend much of our time in Search – not to begin with anyway. But when we do, what is it we are looking for?

The best I can come to is a sense of some very subtle, occasional contact between the living part of myself, the essential 'me' and 'something', usually quite inaccessible, call it my higher parts if you like, the God within me. When, very rarely, this occurs, it is unmistakable, a flash of insight, understanding, of discovery – and then I lose it again.

This is the nature of Search and Need and all the other camping grounds we shall come to. Although we get to know them quite well and think we have left them behind, actually we never leave them. We are constantly coming back. We can keep the moment, but we cannot keep the state. The mystery, the summons in Search is that, even when you have found it, made the contact, been blest with the momentary insight, you lose it again. These pearls are not for nothing. They have to be paid for with effort. And the effort is so to live our lives that we remain open to make this connection and, having made it, to remake it – not to repeat it – for it is always new.

So, in a way, our situation has hardly changed. Before we came to Search, we were discontented, frustrated at the endless futility of life. We were in prison and all that mattered was escape. Now, as we ponder in Search it all begins to look more complicated than when we first began. But this cannot be helped. It is the nature of the human condition. We all want something for nothing, Heaven on a plate, and it simply isn't on.

And while we have been pondering on all this, mulling it over, we suddenly find we have moved. We have come to a new place, and seen that all that is important is whether we *choose* to put ourselves in a position to make efforts or not. We have come to the point of choice. Choice is a very important camping ground – and more difficult to get to than you'd think.

III CHOICE

Choice occupies a commanding position. It stands on a rise at the edge of the plain. There are foothills beyond and, far off, the mountain, wreathed in cloud. Choice is where we actually start the safari and put on our boots. But as I have already said, it is a difficult place to get to. Why?

We think we are always free to choose; but do we? Can we? I am going to suggest to you that we don't, that we have become quite mechanized in everything we do so that, confronted with alternatives, we *think* we choose but actually always follow our 'usual' path, which we 'like' and to which we are accustomed, and have no choice at all.

I dare say this idea will put you 'up in arms', as we say, and you will protest that we are always choosing, that we can do whatever we like, that we have 'free will' and so on. Certainly we *can* choose, but, in general, we don't.

Now there is only one way to verify this and that is to watch ourselves. If we do this honestly, sincerely and over a long time – for you can't check it otherwise – you will be surprised at first and later on, maybe, appalled, shocked, at the extent to which we are all quite automatic. We think and act and react according to our own pattern, as inevitably as a typewriter can only type or a pump pump. We cannot do anything else. We endlessly repeat ourselves.

But, I can hear you say, this is a terrible philosophy. You want me to believe I am no more than a machine, a robot? If it was true there would be no hope for me.

I reply that seeing it, observing it again and again is the beginning of hope – for you, for me, for all of us.

Why? Because it means that progressively as you accept it, you will be bound to see the reality of your situation and it is only a step from that to finding the determination to change it.

People have always had the idea that they can choose, that there are different paths through life; but if we face ourselves it seems there is only one path for each of us, automatic, predetermined. Choice is a mockery.

But, wait a minute. Let's dig a bit deeper. Suppose we have different states – and, after all, we know we *do* have different states – suppose there are states in which we can choose and others in which we cannot? Suppose that to choose we must stir out of our usual, automatic, sleeping state – for that is what it amounts to – and wake up to the fact that there really are different paths, there really is yes and no, life and death, then – what is our choice? What are we choosing between?

You see why I said Choice was a difficult place to find?

I suggest to you, as an idea to ponder over, that the choice is not between different outside paths, the alternatives that seem to present themselves; the choice is really between different people inside ourselves, one of which can choose one way and another its opposite.

Now this, to me, is a mind-blowing idea and it leads us straight on to the next stretch of country, which is called the Many-I-States.

IV THE MANY-I-STATES

This stretch of country I have called the Many-I-States is a very large area. It lies between the plain and the mountain and it is all difficult country. The tracks through it are overgrown. Maps are hard to come by. Many never get through it. Without a guide it is easy to get lost. But it is not 'new' country. It was discovered long ago. In the Gospels there is an almost perfect description of it.

It was in the country of the Gadarenes where this man came to meet Jesus who is described as 'unclean'. He lived 'in the tombs' – that is among dead things. He did what he liked. Nobody could tame him. Sometimes he was 'in the mountains' – exalted. Sometimes he was depressed – back in the tombs again. He was always 'crying' – calling attention to himself and 'cutting himself with stones' – that is, harming himself by his own actions.

When he met the possibility of a new kind of life in the person of Jesus, he would have nothing to do with it. 'What have I to do with Thee?' he asked. Leave me alone.

'Torment me not.' Looking into him, Jesus saw there was not just one 'unclean spirit', but a host of them. 'My name is legion, for we are many,' they said and, for the man's sake, He permitted them to go out of him and enter into a herd of swine – 2000 strong – who rushed down the steep place into the sea and were destroyed.

The destruction of these 'unclean spirits', these different 'I's in the man, 2000 of them, completely changed him and when people came and saw him 'clothed and in his right mind', they couldn't believe it.

This is not an account of a madman returned to sanity, as we usually think of it. It is a picture of you and me, normal, ordinary, decent people. Like the man we are at the mercy of everything around us, 'possessed', intolerant, self-willed, indignant at the least criticism, and nobody is going to tame us or tell us what to do. We don't want to be 'tormented', we don't want to know.

And these 'unclean spirits', what are they? They are our different 'I's which, bundled up together, appear to the world as our personality. Can you begin to recognize them? The 'I' that is always right. The 'I' that likes to be smiled at. The indignant 'I'. The greedy 'I'. The self-pitying 'I'. If we look at ourselves, even for an hour or two, we shall see them, by the dozen, each of them speaking as if they were all of us.

I said at the beginning that this story was an *almost* perfect description of these Many-I-States and I said it because among all these different 'I's there are one or two that are *not* 'evil spirits'. Their voices are quiet and not easily heard, but they are those who, if they could begin to have some influence over the rest, might lead us to the state of being 'clothed and in our right mind'.

We are not so lucky as that man who had the power of Jesus to heal him 'in the twinkling of an eye'. We have to do it ourselves and we cannot, in fact, drive these 'I's out of us. But we can tame them, or begin to try to, so that we control them and they do not, as they do at present, control us. That is a sort of beacon to steer on in this uncharted country.

V A STORY

Everything we do is done at the expense of something else.
If we garden, there's no time for golf. If we go painting
we can't read. To choose concentrates, but it also excludes
and because of the nature of these Many-I-States in which
we are travelling, it isn't easy. Here is another story to
throw some light on the difficulty of our situation.

There is a ship at sea. It is in distress because the crew
have mutinied. They have trussed up the captain and the
officers and thrown them in the hold. *They* know how to run
the ship and they'll take no orders from anyone. But once
the ship is theirs the difficulties begin. They cannot agree
on a course. Some want to go north, others south, some are
for heaving-to, some for running before the wind. The truth
is they have no idea where they are going; but being a self-
willed lot, none of them will admit it. They all start fighting
for the wheel. One after another they seize it, set their own
course, and a moment later it is wrenched from their grasp
and some other crew member takes over. Such is the
confusion that even those who know nothing of navigation
start to butt in. The cook comes up from the galley and
the chief engineer leaves the engines to look after themselves.
In a word, chaos reigns. As the course is always being
changed, small wonder if the ship never gets anywhere. If
this goes on she will certainly founder.

But this ship is in luck because two or three of the crew
are more reasonable and persuade the others to establish
some sort of order. They know no more than the rest, but
at least they can get the cook back in the galley and the
engineer down below. To get the ship functioning normally
is already a change for the better.

After some time these sensible members of the crew
manage to release an officer. He is an educated man and
they begin to follow his instructions. He can use a sextant
and take sun sights. He knows the location of the radio
stations that are all the time calling the ship. So soon they
know where they are and where they are going. It is wonderful to have an aim and steer a course.

What is the situation on your ship? Is it the same as on mine? I must confess that I am still in difficulties, for although I've managed to get a bit of order and an officer to help us all, I do find the crew unruly and have to watch carefully all the time for fear the mindless stupidity of the old days should come back.

And as for the captain, well, the ship's not really in good enough trim to expect him to return to the bridge and take charge – yet. Most of the crew want it now; but the demands he would make are beyond us at present, I think. But, little by little, if we increase our efforts, the day may come when we can go to him to beg his forgiveness and ask him to take charge again.

In the Many-I-States there can never be harmony; but our aim, our direction, is towards a state higher up the mountain where these 'I's all know each other and can act as one.

VI INFLUENCE

This idea that we are not 'all of a piece', but a bundle of often contradictory people, each of which bobs up to the surface in response to some outside stimulus, speaks for the whole of us and then disappears, is strange and, at first, unacceptable.

We have all been brought up to think of ourselves as a person, a 'whole', subject to 'moods' of course, but essentially monolithic, one. Our multiplicity, our contradictions, escape us. We have, in fact, built up a special mechanism to prevent us seeing them. Occasionally this breaks down, when we blush, for instance, it is because we catch ourselves seeing two people in us at the same time, one of which, say, loves something, while the other pretends not to.

I can't expect you to get hold of this idea, more than theoretically, at first. But try to remain open to it, try to watch your behaviour – it is easier to see it in strong situations – and you may notice that when we are angry, we are all anger – there is nobody else there. Ten minutes later we meet a friend and we are all pleasure. Our angry 'I' has

completely vanished and, if we happen to remember i
later, another observant 'I' will point out how ridiculou
it was to get so upset. So it goes, all day long and, as you
begin to see it, you will be amazed and maybe horrifiec
at the way each 'I' takes the centre of the stage, speaks fo
the whole of us and a moment later is gone. But how anc
why do these different 'I's keep on appearing and disappearing? Look up and you will see where we have got to.
We are in the shadow of a mountain called Influence.

Influences overshadow our lives. It can be said that we are
nothing but the results of influences. Parents, friends
teachers, our environment, even the latitude and longitude
in which we live, all mould us into the sort of people we are
All these influences, especially in childhood, are fed intc
our personal computers, stirred up, scrambled and emerge
as our own personality.

Our read out is the product of our own influence bank.
We frown or smile, agree or argue as a result of these read
outs, which we call memory, and each new experience, a
it happens, is fed into our computer and reinforces o
modifies our subsequent reactions.

Earlier on I was suggesting to you that, normally, we
don't choose, but freewheel through situations on ou
computers. To choose we have to wake up and use highe
faculties which are not the mechanical action and reaction
of sleeping life.

We cannot escape influences; but we can choose them –
if we want. Now, at this moment, you are reading these
lines I have written so that you are under my influence.
In a short while you might be under the influence of the
radio or television, your wife, the telephone or the weather.

And beyond all this is the conundrum of 'interest', why
one man wants to be a pianist and another a mountaineer
Our 'slant', which does not depend wholly on influences, bu
on our genes, our heredity, our type, our psyche. Often thi
slant is buried and that is why, sometimes, we reach ou
unknowingly, and come, unexpectedly, on safaris like thi
into the mysteries of our inner life.

VII SPECIMENS

I suppose many of you may think it a bit fanciful to call
this section a Safari. For, after all, a safari is an exciting
trip to discover the haunts of all sorts of strange, shy speci-
mens we never see and observe them 'in the wild'. Compared
with that our human society all seems so commonplace,
so familiar, we hardly give it a glance.

But as soon as we begin to *look*, nobody, believe me, is
such a shy, secret creature as your best friend. You may
know he has a temper, or she is lazy, as you know a lion
roars or a sloth hangs about; but beyond those rudimentary
recognizable traits, you know nothing. Those nearest and
dearest to us, what drives them, what are true springs of
their natures? We hardly know.

This is partly because of our own egoism. Everything is
orientated to me. *My* point of view is all I care about. And
it is also partly because we have no diagrams, no maps,
no working plans to help us to see what we are. We don't
really know how we function, and therefore we have no
idea how others function. If I really understood myself, I
should have little difficulty in understanding others. Here
is the problem. Nobody is so wild, shy and elusive as myself.
But I take myself for granted. I don't know. I don't care.
I don't look. And yet who is so wonderful as myself? Long
ago we all fell in love with ourselves, like a girl of sixteen.
It wasn't a question of merit, it was sheer infatuation. We
took one look at ourselves and – whoops! – we were up on
cloud nine – and we've been there ever since.

So I make no apologies for saying we are on safari and I
must add that if you want to join in you must come down
off that cloud and sneak along in the undergrowth keeping
your eyes open. What I point out to you is little, what I
open for you to find out for yourselves is much.

For instance, I have just written about the great mountain
called Influence and spoke of the enormous part it played in
our lives; but what about the obverse? Do I always respond
to influences or do I reject them, and, if so, why?

Do you see the vista opening up? Are influences very

strong or am I very weak, very malleable, to be impressed
by them? I never question. If Mrs Smith says X is a liar and
tomorrow Mr Jones tells me, very confidentially, he has
discovered X is a liar, then, from that time on, it's fixed
X is a liar! Such is my weakness, my *suggestibility*, I constantly lap up all sorts of rumour, all sorts of nonsense. That
is what propaganda is about.

Where am I in all this? I must stand my ground. Be
active, not passive. And that opens another question, what
is it to be active? You think Mr Roustabout is active because
he is all the time on the go, making decisions, attending
meetings, throwing his weight about? I tell you he is as
passive as a rabbit. He simply has a sharp reactive apparatus. People feed him problems and he comes up with the
answers, as passively as a computer. Active indeed!

Active is what proceeds from me. My own. Passive is what
is reflected from me. So – what am I?

VIII ANATOMY

What am I? What are we? I mean what do we consist of,
how are we put together? Not just physically, you understand – head, body and legs – but what is the shape of our
psychological anatomy, so to speak?

There seem to be four separate parts which together make
up the whole. First, there is our head, where all our dreams,
associations and thoughts are centred; second there is the
place where everything that reaches us through our senses
from the outside, our feelings, are concentrated; and third
there is our body, our basic chassis, so to speak; lastly there
is the combined outcome of these three parts put together,
which we have the habit of calling 'I'.

In order that we should be able to focus all this a bit more
clearly, Gurdjieff, my teacher, proposes an analogy. All
these four components of our personal functioning, he says,
can very well be compared with that organization for
carrying passengers, consisting of a cart, a horse and a
driver. The cart represents our body, the horse our feelings,
and the driver our head, while the owner, sitting in the cart,

or carriage, and deciding where to go, is what we call 'I'.

That is how it should be if all was well with us. But, alas, such as we are, the carriage has no owner. It has become a horse-drawn taxi, plying for hire, into which any chance passer-by can jump, order it off in any direction and leave it where it happens to have got to.

The first thing that strikes us in this wonderful analogy is the disparity between the cart, horse and driver. Their food, their education, the care they need, are all quite different. Yet they are inseparable. They depend on one another. They have to work together. How are they to understand, to communicate with one another?

If you ponder on it, you will find so many questions. For instance, if the horse does not understand English, how can the driver tell it anything beyond right, left and stop? The driver, our cabby, has never been taught how to look after the cart properly, so what can you expect – it is always in for repairs? How should it be properly greased? How should the horse – our feelings – be fed? And then the links. What are the shafts that connect the horse to the cart – that is the feelings with the body? What are the reins, by which the head – the driver – tries to control the horse, our feelings?

Gurdjieff sees modern man as a caricature of the real thing. A stylish carriage, tarted up to the nines, harnessed to a broken-down, starving horse and, sitting on the box, an unshaven, sleepy cabby, padded out to make himself more important, wearing a top hat like Rockefeller with a giant chrysanthemum in his buttonhole.

Is it so wide of the truth? Our puffed-up heads, so proud of all we think we know. Our jaded, demoralized feelings, so starved they will accept any kind of depravity, brutality and shame, without even a kick. Our bodies constantly in and out of the repair shop.

Of what use is such a turn-out? Who would want to own it? Where is the 'I'?

IX CART, HORSE AND DRIVER

Cart, Horse and Driver! It might almost be the name of a pub. But, anyway, half-way through our Safari, it's a good place to pause for a bit for, from it, we get a wonderful view of those Many-I-States, through which we are making our way.

The first thing we notice when we begin to look at ourselves in this way, as consisting of our bodies – the cart, our feelings – the horse, and the coachman – our heads, is that, finally, everything depends upon the horse. If our horse won't move, nothing moves. On the other hand, if our feelings run away – as in madness or hysteria – the whole lot can be wrecked. Our heads, sitting on the box, directing, as they think, the rest of us, can coax, threaten, reason till they are blue in the face; but if our feelings are not engaged, nothing happens. We can see this, not only in our personal lives, but in every treaty, conference, summit since the world began. Reason is powerless alone and when feelings come in, we are lucky indeed if the direction we move in was what our heads intended.

Our feelings are the most mysterious, unaccountable and lonely part of us. Half the time we are ashamed of them, beating them, squashing them, pretending they don't exist and if anyone does happen to fondle this poor horse of ours or show it the least affection, it is ready to gallop to the ends of the Earth for them. A handful of hay is worth a bale of straw, which is all it usually gets for food.

And this head of ours, this bleary-eyed, unshaven cabby in his padded coat and buttonhole, how does he live? Well, mostly hob-nobbing with his buddies about the news of the day or the talk of the town. Inveterately lazy, he does almost nothing for his horse and cart. As long as they keep going, what does he care? What he likes best of all is the shelter where he can get a good tuck in and dream.

The carriage, our body, was designed to work, to carry loads over rough roads. The whole system of its greasing depends on the jolting it gets from such conditions. But on modern asphalt it gets stiff and rusts. Parts get out of order or drop off – and they are not easy to replace. Our cart needs proper attention for, after all, the whole equipage exists to draw it – or rather the owner who should be sitting in it. By itself it can do nothing: it is dragged after the rest of us. But we take it for granted. We have little idea of how it works.

'A horse! A horse! My kingdom for a horse!' So cried the unseated king and we might all well echo the cry – for imagine how it might be!

A vigorous high-stepping mare, a smart coachman understanding his horse so well he hardly needs whip or reins, and in the trim springy gig, the proud owner going about his business.

And who is he, this owner?

He is the man whose life ambition has been to own such a spanking turn-out. He has worked for it, paid for it. He cares for it, loves it, and he has a right to for it is – himself! He owns it. He is the Master. He is 'I', a Man – not in quotation marks.

X HEAD BRAIN

Brain is a very common word. When we say: he is clever or vague or cunning or inventive, it is a way of describing his type of brain. But what is a brain?

We have been thinking about the three parts of ourselves where different functions are seated – our heads, our emotions and our bodies – or better to say the instinctive motor centre which activates our bodies.

These three parts of us, sometimes called the Lower Centres, varied as they are, have one thing in common, they are all focal points, centres, brains, where different kinds of experience are received and stored.

The sensitivity and complexity of our receiving and filing mechanisms are astonishing. Now that we have begun to build our own fumbling computers, we are realizing the miraculous nature of the ones we were born with.

Let us start by having a look at our head, our third

brain. It exists only in man and is, in fact, what differentiates us from the rest of the earthly creation. It is the seat of Reason, that is to say, the ability to compare abstracts, to set up hypotheses, to formulate plans, to question, to remember – all of which faculties – I sometimes think, luckily for them – are not possessed by other creatures. Our heads create all our possibilities. Our heads can choose.

Our heads also have upper floors; but we spend nearly all our time on the ground floor. This is where our associations, our files, our miraculous card index are stored. This is where we can put all sorts of things together in our own way; but, notice, all this is a reaction to *what is already stored there*, our material. If we have no material on a subject, we go blank; we don't know. All our lives we are having experiences, recording them, and living according to their influence on us. That is why it is said: Man is a machine controlled by external influences.

This is man at his lowest, living at second hand on the frozen food of what he has already collected. It is the way most of us live. But there are upper floors in our thinking apparatus which we can reach – sometimes. Flashes of insight, moments when some thought appears full grown, nothing to do with association, but so compulsive in its clarity that it illuminates a whole situation or solves a problem. This is often called genius or inspiration. It is nothing of the kind. It is simply our heads, really working, really thinking; but, such as we are, we cannot go upstairs at will.

Don't forget the analogy of cart, horse and driver. Our heads alone can drive us. Whether they know where to go or not, they sit on the box and drive. As we are taxis, plying for hire, we go wherever the 'fare' tells us to. But if we could begin to give up such an aimless job, struggle to find our own way, our own truth, our own understanding, everything would be different.

And what is the struggle?

It is to go on puzzling at questions we cannot answer. Why have I been given life? To what purpose? To what end?

Head cannot answer alone; but it can drive us towards the answer.

XI HOW TO FEED THE HORSE

Feelings are the most mysterious, difficult parts of ourselves to get at. In the last few hundred years we have educated ourselves to believe that everything can be worked out by the head and we take such pride in our mental processes we think they can solve everything. They can't. They don't. We are kidding ourselves.

In thought there are paths, roads, maps – a logical progression. This is what we like. We can think our way from A to B. But there is no road from fear to courage, from pride to shame, from generosity to greed. It is a total change. A jump. Feeling is a state, not a process. The horse is a totally different creature from the driver. His needs are different. He does not express himself in words. The driver has to feed him. Nobody else can. And yet the driver neither knows nor cares what he ought to eat. So he feeds him processed food, frozen food. It is easier and cheaper.

This food comes in packets labelled 'if', 'could', 'should', and so on. 'If I had more money, I should feel happier', 'I could have killed him, laughing at me like that', 'We should do more for those who suffer'. Our behaviour, our moral code, what we ought to feel, how we ought to behave, is largely made up of the conventional morality of the time. But we do not really feel it. Far from it. So we do not feed the horse.

But how should we feed him? It is not easy to answer. And yet you may begin to see that it is absolutely vital, basic, to find out. For, finally, as I have said, everything depends on the state of the horse. If there are hills to climb, it is he who must climb them. How can he find the strength if he is not fed?

I wonder if you feel a bit baffled by questions like this? It is an unaccustomed way of thinking about ourselves, about life. It confuses us. We don't understand and tend to reject the whole attitude. I know I have stood before this question of how to feed my horse for years and even now I only understand a tiny bit of it.

You see only the owner knows how to feed the horse. And the owner isn't there. This is the problem. Only he has acquired the means to buy the necessary food. But, because we have let the whole vehicle get into such a dilapidated, run-down state, he's not going to waste it on us unless we can smarten up a bit. But sometimes, out of pity, he comes by, tells the driver to brace up and gives a handful of oats to the horse.

And maybe these brief wonderful visits start me thinking: how could I tempt him to come more often? For, if he did, I know that everything would be different.

For the owner, I need hardly tell you, is the representative of the Creator in us, our Conscience, the chief directing lever of our wholeness, our only hope to drive in the right direction.

And what is the right direction?

I don't need to worry about that. If, in my devotion and desire to serve the owner, I get myself straightened out, he will take care of that. My business is only to drive . . . and drive . . . and drive . . .

XII THE CART

We mustn't leave Cart, Horse and Driver without examining the cart – our bodies. In a way they seem the most get-at-able part of us. Thoughts and feelings are abstract, body is concrete, solid. But it is difficult to accept the idea that our bodies, like the cart, are dragged along, passively, behind us. We think of them as very active. We don't see that the activity is not in the body itself, but in what it is put to. *I* want to walk. *I* want to dig. *I* want to climb. *I* want it: my body follows, obeys.

We only see our bodies in an active role when they have needs of their own, such as thirst or hunger, or sometimes in some special need as, for instance, pregnant women who must have oranges or that anaemic poacher who *had* to eat the livers of the rabbits he snared.

And this leads us to a complication, if we think of these various parts of ourselves as having control centres, brains, then, upon examination, we discover there are two such centres in our bodies. One of these we may call our 'moving' centre, our habits, our automatism by which we carry out all sorts of complex actions we have learned or been taught and, closely allied with it, another centre, the root of everything, our instinctive centre.

What wonders go on in the chemical factory of our bodies! Ten thousand interlocking processes are continuously at work to preserve that harmonious balance we call health. Don't tell me that all this happens 'by itself'. There is a formidable intelligence at work here – yet we know almost nothing of it.

All this is given; but much else is acquired. We *learn* to walk, to balance on a bicycle, to drive a car. Gradually, as we grow up, we acquire a way of doing things that is all our own. By the time we are adult, we cannot behave in any other way. We are, as we say, the 'slaves of habit'. Try brushing your teeth with your left hand. Try walking with your left toe turned in and you will soon see your resistance to change of habit. Our whole approach to life gradually becomes fixed, and is there for life. It is the way we move, our moving centre. And all this also goes on by itself, automatically.

Who is driving the car while you hold an intelligent conversation about the political situation or last night's play? Who is steering, changing gear, judging distance? Not you. Not your head. If you try to *think*, now I must brake, now I must change down, you won't be able to exceed 5 m.p.h. and be had up for obstructing the traffic! Leave it to the moving centre. It is far quicker and more efficient than that head of yours of which you are so proud!

Try to hang on to this wonderful analogy. It is a true picture of all of us and the more you think about it, the more you will find. Try to find the means to withdraw from the endless chatter and small talk of daily life at least for a time every day and so make room for such valuable things.

Believe me that can be the beginning of a new life for all of us.

XIII THE PONDER TREE

Has this Safari we've been on got us anywhere? Let's sit down in the shade of the ponder tree and recap.

We only seem to have come across two ideas really. First, that we are not one person, but many. Inside me is a legion of different people, all of whom speak in my name. That is a new and basic idea which you will not find in standard works on psychology. Second, that we have several different control centres or brains, each of which takes care of its own particular type of impression – thoughts, feelings, habits and so on.

Now if you begin to ponder on these two ideas and gradually begin to accept them, even theoretically, that alone will be a big change. You will begin to see the way we humans are constructed and many things will be clearer to you than they ever were before.

But, of course, it is very difficult to see all this in oneself. It is far easier to observe it in others. So although the goal in all this is *self* observation, it is permissible, to begin with, to watch and listen to others. You will see amusement, vanity, indignation, irritation, sex, all taking charge of your friends and acquaintances, before your very eyes! It is fascinating. Here is the human mechanism at work. This is how it goes.

Fascinating, but alarming too. For it doesn't take long to realize: This is me! I am like that!

There are people within me who have never heard of these ideas – and don't want to. There are 'I's that ask nothing better than to gossip and chatter all day over trivial things. So it happens that only occasionally do we come back to those within us which, as the Gospels put it, 'hunger and thirst after righteousness'.

So the question arises: How can I come back more often? How can I find those elusive 'I's which are all too easily submerged under the hurly-burly of everyday life? All I can do is give you some pointers.

We are like weathercocks, we swing around before every breeze that blows. But were it not for these swings there would be no hope for us, for we should never come round to the direction that is searching for these things. Our swings are our ruination and our salvation at the same time. All we can do is to make a desperate effort to damp them down. And the best way to do this is to set apart a time, morning and evening, to withdraw from the world and turn in another direction.

Do not be dismayed if, as soon as you try to be quiet, you find every sort of reason to stop it. All your other 'I's, all the momentum of your ordinary life, clamours for your attention. And the more you refuse, the more they shout. So, within seconds, you are off, chattering, arguing, criticizing, justifying – as you always do.

This is a well-known human predicament and every serious religious teaching has different weapons to help people to fight what one of the early Christian Fathers called 'the dark-faced Ethiopians'.

So we must be up and on our way to choose our weapons.

XIV SELF-DEFENCE

If we could understand the terrible waste of our lives, how we continually turn and turn around insignificant interests and insignificant aims, if we could see what we are losing, we might wake up to the fact that only one thing is serious, to escape from the general law, to be free! What can be serious to a man condemned to death? Only one thing: how to save himself, how to escape. Nothing else matters.

But to escape is not so easy. An unprepared escape will not succeed. A man must take stock of circumstances, assess the hazards, have a thorough knowledge of the prison, trust his leader, test his friends and then, taking his life in his hands, say his prayers, and go!

This is what this Safari is all about. It is a recce to examine the nature of the terrain, to assess the difficulties, the obstacles, to decide whether escape is possible, whether

the risk is worthwhile. Many will prefer to remain where
they are. The prison is known, even comfortable in its way.
Why take such risks? But others, to whom freedom is life,
think only of their aim and ask for weapons for their self-
defence.

The first weapon is quiet. All the energy I need for my
escape is frittered away in a continual chasing after this and
that and the other. Worries, fears, anxieties, doubts, hopes,
desires, all these fill up my life. I have no room for anything
else. They rob me of all my energies, all my hopes of
anything real. I fight them with my determination to
find quiet – at first for a little time each day, later for
always.

Quietness is not a passive state. It is not just lolling in a
chair and doing nothing. It has to be fought for. As soon as
I try it, I am assailed by the whole momentum of my ordinary
life, which is not used to quiet, which hates silence. So
to be quiet, I must be intensely alert, if I am to ward off
these enemies desiring my dispersion, my destruction.

What do I find when I try it? I find it is impossible.
I can't do it. I can't 'make my mind a blank'. It doesn't
work. And for a very simple reason. Nature abhors a
vacuum. My machine, my normal functions, are designed
to associate. That is their job. If I am to quiet them, I
must give them something to do. Not perhaps what they
want to do; but what they can be persuaded to put up with.
It is a trick to stop them frittering away all my energies.

All religions propose different techniques to meet this
difficulty. One that I have followed for thirty years is to place
my attention in each of my limbs in turn and go round my
body, arm, leg, leg; arm; from shoulder to finger, from
thigh to toe, trying intently to relax my muscles which – I
soon find – are tense and difficult to let go. All my life, for
this time, is within my limbs, persistently insisting, relaxing
them little by little. And so I begin to be quiet.

Of course I fail! My mind takes off in all directions.
But I have my weapon: my *attention*. I come back.

So we arrive at a strange, simple realization. The first
step towards the Kingdom of Heaven lies in my power to

control my attention. Unless I learn to control my attention, nothing is possible for me.

XV POINT OF DEPARTURE

Our Safari is almost at its end – and it seems we have hardly begun. So much remains to be explored. We have been so busy looking at ourselves, we haven't had time to sit and look up at the stars and try to discover our place, our purpose in the wheeling magnificence of the Creation. That must be for another time.

Still we have made the first steps into this strange unexpected country and I have offered you material upon which you can begin to draw – if you wish – a new picture of your own nature. Not something framed and finished. Just a sketch which you can add to, fill in, as you yourself discover more. Look and you will see your perpetual fluctuations – how you love what you hate and hate what you love. Look and you will see how your thought is always at the mercy of your feelings, how you cannot escape the ruts of your habits.

The most precious antiseptic in every effort we make to cut into our own insides is that we begin to stop lying to ourselves. We begin to face the truth, not always so flattering. I am what I am. At first the idea of such an operation seems frightening, but as, little by little, some of our imagination is cut away, we begin to feel healthy, clean, free of all the tricks, subterfuges and deceptions. To live in truth is freedom.

Of course what we see will not disappear just because we have seen it. No such luck. In fact, if we had time to push on further, we should see how our work is not to cut out all those parts of us we do not like; but to accept them, relate to them, tame them, forgive them, so that when, at last, we set foot on the mountain, we can say: What I know, the whole of me knows. I am all I am. But that's a long trek. Far ahead.

And talking of treks. Do you know the fable of the ant who wanted to go to Mecca? He was a good ant and he'd discharged all his obligations to his fellows in the nest, so one day, when they saw him rolling up his things, they stopped and asked him what he was up to.

'I am going to Mecca,' he said.

At first they didn't believe him. There was the whole Sahara between, thousands of miles of it. The clever ones started to explain the distance, the impossibility . . . But our ant went on packing.

Then they remonstrated with him: 'Why do you want to go? It's ridiculous. Isn't it good enough here, in the nest, with all your friends? Why on earth do you want to go out, alone, into all those unknown places?' But the ant smiled and just went on packing.

By now all the others were really alarmed. 'Have you gone crazy?' they said to him. 'Listen. There are no roads, no water. The sun will burn you to a cinder. There are wild beasts too, snakes, tigers, hyenas. Stay here with us. Don't be a fool!'

But our heroic ant, for we must conclude he was such, swung his bundle up over his shoulder and pushed his friends aside.

'I have a desire,' he said, 'to see the Holy Places before I die. It does not matter if the distances are great. It does not matter if there are dangers on the road. It does not matter if the sun burns me up. It does not even matter if I die of thirst and the vultures pick my bones. I put my trust in Allah, the Merciful, the Compassionate. He knows I shall be ON MY WAY!'

Chapter 18

The Heart of the Matter

I

We have now examined the wonderful peace and beauty of Nature, that marvellous equilibrium that she achieves, paradoxically, through everything feeding on everything else, on death being the price of life. We saw how Nature *kills without anger*, to eat, to live, and therefore kills without sin.

Yet we, who are also part of Nature – and some would say the pinnacle of her creation – seem somehow to have lost this harmony, to be out of step with the world in which we live. We see Nature sometimes as a friend, who provides for us and consoles us, sometimes as an enemy to be beaten and plundered; but, in fact, she is beyond all that, perfectly impartial. 'The rain falls on the just and the unjust.' Nature does not take sides.

Then surely we must ask ourselves the question; how is Man different? What makes him an outsider? How is it that he cannot seem to be content with his state, like the rest of the creation?

The answer is that, while remaining an animal, part of Nature, rooted in her laws, he has also been blessed – and cursed – with an additional faculty, unique to him alone, which may be called a head brain, an intelligence. Why he has been so endowed is beyond us. For reasons of His own, God made it so. But we may observe that this faculty of intelligence does not appear to rest in evolution, to have come about by natural selection; but to be of quite a different order, as if it has been bestowed as a Divine gift, something at once wonderful and dangerous, with immense possibilities not open to the rest of creation, thrown out as a sort of gesture or challenge to see what we would make of it.

There are Beings with only one centre, or brain. Such

creatures are rooted in habit and instinct and live by i
These are trees, plants, the vegetable world. There are othe
Beings who have a second centre added, which enable
them to feel. They can care and mate, protect their of
spring, change their environment, move and fight for the
lives. These two categories of one-brained and two-braine
Beings comprise the whole gamut of Nature from the mos
to the oak, from the ant to the elephant.

Superimposed on all this comes Man to whom has bee
added a third brain, the seat of Reason. This is a uniqu
attribute, quite different from instinct or feeling. It enable
us to compare abstracts, speculate, project into the futur
and, at the same time, to collect, categorize, co-ordinate
that is to use the extraordinary faculty of memory.

We have only to look around today to observe — an
indeed to marvel at – the fantastic fruits of this thir
brain, the human intelligence. It ought to, it could, pu
Heaven within our grasp. But somehow, it doesn't seer
to. Why?

II

I am bound to tell you that I approach what I now sa
with the greatest trepidation, for the reason why Man ha
never been able to make full use of this two-pronged gift c
Reason touches the quick, the core of the matter and I ar
very ill-equipped to speak about it.

Every serious religion teaches that Man has two natures
He has one foot in this world and the other – very timidl
and tentatively – in some world above or beyond him
Great teachers have come, down the ages, to persuad
Man to see how much better a life he could lead if he pu
more weight on this other foot and to show him how to se
about it. But, in general, these truths have not 'stuck'
as it were, and have very quickly been forgotten, lost
submerged, and men have reverted to the kind of lif
with which they were familiar and could live more easily
The difficulties, desirable as the goal might be, have alway
been too big for most of us to face.

Giving Man reason enabled him, from time to time, to see where he was going and how he stood in relation to the world about him. Not always. He has his highs, his lows, as the song says. But somewhere among the highs he touched the strain of ambition in himself. Aspiration appeared; the desire to be 'better'. This reaching out towards a part of him he did not understand, called spiritual growth, filled him with visions of a more perfect state. Since those he saw about him who had attained this state, or were on their way to it, radiated wisdom and peace, it appeared a desirable aim and called him. What had they got that he had not got? He determined to find out.

Now we must clearly understand that such an ambition is an absolutely personal matter. Nobody else is in the least interested. Life does not need it. In fact 'ordinary' life will do everything it possibly can to maintain the *status quo*, the comfortable, easy life we are all used to. The great mass of humanity live quite satisfactory lives without any of these obscure desires. To long for the Kingdom of Heaven is not an educational requirement. It is a pearl of great price and very few of us can afford it even if we pay as we earn.

It is said that life is set up as it is to provide us with opportunities for struggle. Life is a fight and our merit, when we come to the end of it, is how we have struggled. If we have struggled and not made much of a job of it, we may realize how much respect is due to those who, patiently and persistently, struggle towards their own inner growth, for of all struggles, this is the most arduous and desirable. But what is the essence of this struggle?

You realize by now, I expect, that I am a terrible procrastinator. I simply do not want to come to this point. For the point, the nub of it all, is so simple, so obvious, once you see it and so totally unacceptable, ridiculous, outrageous, if you do not, that I just don't want to put you – or myself – to the test, in case we should lose each other.

III

Whatever you are doing at this moment, let me ask you a simple question: Where are your hands? Now. Where are they? Give them your attention. How are they lying? What are they doing? Until a moment ago, when I asked you the question, did you know even that you had hands? Mentally of course you know it; but as *your hands*, living, part of you, I suggest that you – and I, all of us – exist taking them absolutely for granted, unconscious, unaware of them.

And now? Ten seconds later. Where are they? You see? We have forgotten. We do not know. And we live like this! Totally disconnected from ourselves. What goes for our hands, goes for our feet, our speech, our actions, our thoughts, they all go on, as it were, by themselves, without our participation. It works. It walks. It speaks. It argues, fights, dies – automatically, as it had been conditioned to do. 'I' have no part in it.

Now this is no fantasy. It is a fact: a verifiable fact. Try it. Every time we come back to ourselves, we cannot fail to see that, up to that moment, we have been disconnected with our source, our 'I'. Something hurries about all day long in a sort of dream which seems real, but isn't. Something agrees, disagrees, promises in my name, a thousand times a day, without once referring it to me. I was not present. I did not exist. This has been called the 'terror of the situation'. Maybe you don't understand, don't see it; but, once you see it – and its implications – nothing will ever be quite the same to you again. For all the evil in life arises directly out of the fact that our existence withers away, day after day, unconsciously, automatically, mechanically. We are never there. We forget ourselves. The root of all sin is this forgetfulness. Did not Jesus cry out from the agony of the Cross 'Father, forgive them, for *they do not know what they are doing*'?

Come back to your hands. Where are they now? Look at them. Try to get inside them. Sense them. They belong to you. How miraculous they are! What wonders have flowed from the human hand! Keep your attention on them. Now . . . Just for a moment . . . You see? As long as you are connected with yourself, you are alive in a new way. It feels different. I am there! I and my hands . . .

I need not live mechanically, as if I were asleep. I can wake up, to myself, to life. It is not impossible. I need not snore away my days in dreams, in fantasies. If I can connect with myself, remember myself, this way, for a moment, I can do it for an hour, a day, always perhaps . . .

Alas, we have been conditioned to forget. So this is the longest and most arduous struggle in life. Almost impossible. Nevertheless, I have shown you the heart of the matter. This is El Dorado. Respect the quiet, patient ones who try. Truly they bear our most sacred hope. For, as long as we ignore, repudiate or ridicule this central truth, the world is doomed to remain the way it is. Well . . . Do we like the way it is?

Also available in Fount Paperbacks

What is Real in Christianity?
DAVID L. EDWARDS

The author strips away the legends from Jesus to show the man who is real, relevant and still fascinating. A clear, confident statement of Christian faith taking account of all criticisms.

The First Christmas
H. J. RICHARDS

Can one really believe in the seventies in such improbable events as the Virgin Birth, the shepherds and the angels, the Magi and the star in the East? Are they just fables? This book suggests that they might be the wrong questions to ask, and may even prevent the reader from arriving at the deeper issues. What these deeper issues are is here explained with clarity, simplicity and honesty.

Wrestling with Christ
LUIGI SANTUCCI

'This is a most unusual book, a prolonged meditation of the life of Christ using many changing literary forms, dialogue, description, addresses to Christ, passages of self-communing. It is written by a Christian passionately concerned that everyone should know Jesus Christ.'   *Catholic Herald*

Journey for a Soul
GEORGE APPLETON

'Wherever you turn in this inexpensive but extraordinarily valuable paperback you will benefit from sharing this man's pilgrimage of the soul.'   *Methodist Recorder*

Also available in Fount Paperbacks

Infallible?
HANS KÜNG

'It is clear that this is a book of extreme importance for the future of the Christian Churches as a whole, Küng's analysis, if it is valid, might provide a basis on which the three great branches of Christendom could re-unite.'

Desmond Fisher, Church Times

Why Priests?
HANS KÜNG

An attempt by one of the world's leading brilliant and most controversial theologians to answer in a sympathetic and unswervingly Christian way, the question Why Priests?

Letters to Two Friends 1926-1952
TEILHARD DE CHARDIN

'A deep thinking book about the Jesuit priest-scientist's life and the development of his thought. These letters reflect the turmoils of his thought and the triumph of his Christian reason.'

Guardian

The Spirituality of Teilhard de Chardin
THOMAS CORBISHLEY

In this book Father Corbishley analyses what 'spirituality' meant to Teilhard and his understanding of it can correct many a misapprehension about its real significance.

Also available in Fount Paperbacks

Luther
GERHARD EBELING

'On reading this book one recovers a sense that theology is about what really matters . . . Although it is a deeply serious book it is very readable and deserves a wide public.'
A. D. Galloway, Glasgow Herald

Erasmus of Christendom
ROLAND H. BAINTON

'In this book, which carries lightly and easily the massive Erasmian scholarship of the last half-century, Erasmus comes to life. He speaks for himself and, speaking, reveals himself.'
Hugh Trevor-Roper, Sunday Times

Calvin
FRANCOIS WENDEL

'This is the best introduction to Calvin and his theology that has been written, and it is a work of scholarship which one salutes and admires.'
Professor Gordon Rupp

The Religious Experience of Mankind
NINIAN SMART

In this study of great world religions the author shows that religions grow and change and affect each other just as living organisms do. He points out that one cannot understand human history without knowing something about man's religion.

Also available in Fount Paperbacks

A Historical Introduction to the New Testament
ROBERT GRANT

This splendid book is a New Testament introduction with a difference . . . All students of the New Testament will welcome this original and courageous study.'

Professor James S. Stewart

The Historical Geography of the Holy Land
G. ADAM SMITH

A classic which has fascinated and instructed generations of students. This masterpiece among the vast literature on the Bible . . . will continue to delight readers as well as to inform.'

H. H. Rowley

The Dead Sea Scrolls 1947-1969
EDMUND WILSON

A lucid narrative of the discovery of the scrolls which soon turns into a learned detective story; then an account of the excitement, the consternation and the intrigues.'

V. S. Pritchett, New Statesman

The Gospels and the Jesus of History
XAVIER LEON-DUFOUR

This book is far more than an introduction to the study of the Gospels. With its detailed study of the Gospels and of the other New Testament books it is an excellent introduction to the Christology of the New Testament.' *William Barclay*